Gender and the Israeli-Palestinian Conflict

Syracuse Studies on Peace and Conflict Resolution
Harriet Hyman Alonso, Charles Chatfield, and Louis Kreisberg
Series Editors

Gender and the Israeli-Palestinian Conflict

The Politics of Women's Resistance

SIMONA SHARONI

Syracuse University Press

Library of Congress Cataloging-in-Publication Data
Sharoni, Simona.
    Gender and the Israeli-Palestinian conflict : the politics of
women's resistance / Simona Sharoni.
        p.   cm. — (Syracuse studies on peace and conflict resolution)
    Includes bibliographical references and index.
    ISBN 0-8156-2643-6 (cl : alk. paper). — ISBN 0-8156-0299-5 (pb :
alk. paper)
    1. Women, Palestinian Arab—West Bank—Political activity.
2. Women, Palestinian Arab—Gaza Strip—Political activity.
3. Jewish women—Israel—Political activity.   4. Intifada, 1987–
Participation, Female.   5. Women, Palestinian Arab—Social
role—West Bank.   6. Jewish women—Israel—Social conditions.   7. Sex
role—West Bank.   8. Sex role—Gaza Strip.   9. Sex role—Israel.
10. Feminist theory.   I. Title.   II. Series.
  HQ1728.5.Z8W4773   1995
    305.42′095695′3—dc20   94-32264

Manufactured in the United States of America

Contents

Simona Sharoni is an Israeli feminist and peace activist, who is currently assistant professor of peace and conflict resolution at the American University in Washington, D.C. She holds a Ph.D. in conflict analysis and resolution from George Mason University, and her research has been supported by grants from the American Association of University Women (AAUW), the United States Institute for Peace (USIP), and the John D. and Catherine T. MacArthur Foundation.

Illustrations

Acknowledgments

➔ The first seed for this book was planted about four years ago, at the October 1990 conference of the Consortium On Peace Education Research and Development (COPRED) in Dayton, Ohio. Following my presentation of a paper on the struggles of Palestinian and Israeli-Jewish women against the Israeli occupation, I met Cynthia Maude-Gembler, the executive editor at Syracuse University Press who urged me to send her an outline for a book on women and the Israeli-Palestinian conflict. Since that day, Cynthia has invested a great deal of energy, both emotional and intellectual, in this project. Her personal and professional dedication, limitless faith in me, and unconditional support were instrumental to the completion of this book.

Although the book is quite different both in scope and in format from my doctoral dissertation, it draws primarily on the extensive research I had carried out for my Ph.D. Thus, I would like to acknowledge the encouragement and support of my dissertation committee. In particular, I would to thank Richard Rubenstein, who chaired the committee, for his intellectual and political backing and Linda Forcey for her integrity, dedication, and invaluable advice during different stages of research, writing, and job-searching. Sadly, Jim Laue did not live long enough to see this book published. He was the first who gave me "academic" permission to assert myself as a scholar-activist and encouraged me to be out front about my political commitment.

Fellowships from the Educational Foundation of the American Association of University Women (AAUW) and from the Institute for Intercultural Studies were instrumental during earlier stages of the project. The completion of this manuscript was made possible by a research and writing grant from the United States Institute of Peace. I would also like to acknowledge and thank Amee Shah, my graduate research assistant at the School of International Service, American University, for preparing the index as well as for her assistance in the last stages of the project.

I could not have completed this book, however, without the invaluable personal and political encouragement, and insights of numerous people who gave willingly their time and leant their emotional and intellectual support in the past four years. In the Middle East, my thanks, first and foremost, go to the many women activists in Israel and in the West Bank and Gaza Strip who made this project possible. In Israel, I would like to thank Yvonne Deutsch, Tchia Dov, Yafa Gavish, Ruth Cohen, Hava Keller, Rachel Ostrowitz, Hagar Rovelev, Dalia Sachs, and Hannah Safran. I would also like to acknowledge and thank the staff and volunteers of two Jerusalem-based centers—Challenge and the Alternative Information Center (AIC)—for their political integrity and relentless struggle for a just and lasting resolution of the conflict.

On the Palestinian side, I am especially grateful to Maha Nassar, Assia Habash, and Eileen Kuttab for their time, trust, and numerous illuminating conversations. I also wish to acknowledge the support of women from the Union of Palestinian Women's Association in North America, particularly Camilia Odeh, Maha Jarad and Rabab Abdulhadi. Words only begin to convey the strength, courage, insight, and hope that I have drawn from my personal relationship and collaborative work with Rabab. I would also like to acknowledge Nahla Abdo for her courage and for fruitful collaboration on academic and political projects.

Special heartfelt thanks go to friends and colleagues in the Feminist Theory and Gender Studies section of the International Studies Association (ISA), who have become my major support system in the past four years. I wish to thank Linda Forcey again for introducing me to this exciting network, and Christine Sylvester, Spike Peterson, Anne Sisson Runyan, and Sandra Withworth for their faith in me and in my work and for all that I have learned through my relationships with them. I would also like to acknowledge and thank the COPRED community. In particular, I would like to express my gratitude to Elise Boulding for introducing me to this network, for having faith in my work and for opening so many doors. Special thanks go to my colleagues on the organization's Board of Directors and to Barbara Wein, the executive director of COPRED, for her energy, integrity, and dedication.

In the past two years I have also benefited from interaction with and the support of a number of people associated with the World Order Models Project (WOMP). I would like to thank Saul Mendlowitz for inviting me to be part of this community and Richard Falk for his advice and instrumental support of my research project and job search. In particular, because their political integrity and compassion makes such a difference in the world and in my life, I would like to acknowledge and thank Lester Ruiz and Radmila Nakarada. More personally, I would like to thank Beth Ritterpusch, Nimet Beriker, Peri Pamir, and Peter McGrain for their special friendship and unconditional support and Samya Daoud, Tamar Shechter, Nancy Coffin, Muhammed Abu-Nimer, David Cianto, and Chris Koomey for their affirmation and friendship.

Finally, my deepest thanks and appreciation go to my companion, Steve Niva, for his love, care, emotional support, and intellectual stimulation and for the enormous time and energy he invested in this project. I feel particularly fortunate for the opportunity to learn and grow with someone who shares my political commitment to the struggles for gender equality on one hand and for a just resolution of the Israeli-Palestinian conflict on the other.

Washington, D.C.   Simona Sharoni
August 1994

Abbreviations

CRM	Citizen's Rights Movement
DFLP	Democratic Front for the Liberation of Palestine
GUPW	General Union of Palestinian Women
PFLP	Popular Front for the Liberation of Palestine
PFWAC	Palestine Federation of Women's Action Committees
PLO	Palestine Liberation Organization
PNC	Palestine National Council
PWA	Palestinian Women's Association
UNLU	Unified National Leadership of the Uprising
UPWWC	Union of Palestinian Women's Working Committees
WAO	Women Against the Occupation
WCSW	Women's Committee for Social Work
WILPF	Women's International League for Peace and Freedom
WOFPP	Women's Organization for Women Political Prisoners
UPWA	Union of Palestinian Women's Associations in North America
UPWC	Union of Palestinian Women's Committees
WWC	Women's Work Committee

Gender and the Israeli-Palestinian Conflict

1

Introduction

➤ The outbreak of the Palestinian *intifada*, the popular uprising of Palestinians against the Israeli occupation of the West Bank and Gaza Strip, which began in December 1987, marked a crucial turning point in the political mobilization of many Israeli-Jewish and Palestinian women. The *intifada* was one of the major catalysts behind the change in the magnitude and visibility of women's activism both in Israel and in the West Bank and Gaza Strip. In addition to empowering Palestinian and Israeli-Jewish women to step up their level of political involvement, and creating a new context for alliances across the Israeli-Palestinian divide, the *intifada* brought the struggles of Palestinian and Israeli-Jewish women to the attention of the international community.

Feminist scholars and activists, women peace activists, and sympathetic journalists traveled to Israel, and to the Israeli-occupied West Bank and Gaza Strip, to witness the upsurge in women's political activism and to express solidarity with and lend support to these struggles. The result is a rapidly growing body of literature on Palestinian and Israeli-Jewish women. Based primarily on interviews with Palestinian and Israeli-Jewish women activists, and written for the most part in English, this work has generated mixed responses from women in both communities.

Many women activists were torn between their eagerness to spread the message about their struggles to a wider audience and their uneasiness with being someone's "object of study." Women activists featured in some books and articles were not always pleased with the way they had been described and analyzed, even when they had been consulted and asked to review sections that dealt with their lives. The problem is not generally one of misrepresentation but cuts across a variety of more serious issues. As a Palestinian woman activist pointed out about a recent book written by an American woman sympathetic to the Palestinian women's movement , "the problem was not with what she wrote about me, in fact she did a good job articulating my position. The problem was with the arguments that my quotes were supposed to support and with the broader context that framed the project."[1]

The nature of feminist solidarity and the similarities and differences between the struggles of Palestinian and Israeli-Jewish women and women's political activism in other parts of the world revealed yet another problem area. Although some women were eager to spend hours discussing the applicability of feminist perspectives and interpretations to the Israeli-Palestinian context, others rejected the imposition of what one Israeli-Jewish woman termed "textbook feminism" upon their particular struggles.

Some of these problems stem from the fact that much of the work dealing with the political involvement of Palestinian and Israeli-Jewish women has not been written primarily *for* women activists in the region but rather *about* them. The major impetus has been to provide information about the daily lives and struggles of Israeli-Jewish and Palestinian women to a wider public, outside the Middle East, mainly in Europe and in North America. This emphasis was based on the assumption that such information is likely to counter stereotypes, to raise awareness of the implications of the Israeli-Palestinian conflict for women's lives, and to mobilize broader international support for the struggle against the Israeli occupation and for a just and lasting resolution of the conflict.

Many Palestinian and Israeli-Jewish women activists recognize the importance of this literature and its contribution to their broader struggles. At the same time, there has been a growing consensus, especially among grassroots activists on both sides of the Israeli-Palestinian divide, on the need to document and theorize about women's political struggles from within their own movements. To move in that direction, women in Israel, and in the West Bank and Gaza Strip, have begun to address the relationship between gender issues and other social and political problems in their lives in newsletters, magazines, panel discussions, and local and international conferences. Palestinian women have established a number of women's centers in the West Bank and Gaza Strip, including a Women's Studies program at Birzeit University. Israeli women, on the other hand, are gathering material for a book, written by and for activists, on women's peace activism in Israel since the *intifada*. In addition, they are organizing an international conference on women, war and peace scheduled for December 1994.

This book has been inspired by the urgency and excitement surrounding Palestinian and Israeli-Jewish activists' efforts to document and analyze their struggles from the inside out. But where is the "inside" and who is authorized to represent it? Who frames the issues and sets the boundaries around what can be researched? What are the political implications of addressing certain issues and leaving others aside? The importance of grappling with such questions, which raise issues regarding authorship, identity, representation, and responsibility, cannot be overestimated. At the same time it is important to bear in mind that none of these questions has clear or easy answers.[2] The challenge is to recognize the necessity of continually asking these questions without creating or perpetuating rigid distinctions between self and other, insider and outsider, theory and practice or scholar and activist.

The distinction between *insiders* and *outsiders* represents one way of separating "us" from "them." This distinction has been used to separate people who live in the Middle East from those who do not, feminists from non-feminists and grassroots activists from academic scholars. But the terms *insider* and *outsider*, which are often utilized to establish or undermine authority, authenticity, and credibility, acquire different meanings depending on the context. On the grassroots level in social movements, for example, being an insider may lend credibility and access to privileged information. Within academic circles, on the other hand, attempts to write as an insider, particularly about social movements, are often met with resistance by those who argue that in order to produce "sound and objective scholarship," a scholar must remain an outsider.

This book is written from both an insider's and an outsider's perspective. The decision to write from both perspectives, while refusing all along the rigid distinctions between them, is related to my own fragmented identity and personal/political experiences. I am an insider since I grew up in Israel, lived there most of my adult life, and was active both in the women's movement and in the peace movement prior to and after the outbreak of the *intifada*. At the same time I am an outsider. During the past five years, I have spent more time in the U.S. than in the Middle East, while completing a Ph.D. in Conflict Analysis and Resolution, and engaging in public speaking, local organizing and writing on gender issues and the Israeli-Palestinian conflict.

By writing from both an insider's and an outsider's perspective, I have sought to reach a broad audience, comprised of academics and activists in the Middle East and elsewhere. In addition, this approach enabled me to explore the relationship between theory, research, and practice. Rather than testing the applicability of a given theoretical framework to a particular case study, as is often done in conventional social science studies, I have located my research and theoretical domain within the daily lives and ongoing struggles of Palestinian women in the West Bank and Gaza Strip and Jewish women in Israel, treating the perspectives and strategies of women activists as theories about gender issues, resistance, and the Israeli-Palestinian conflict.

This is a book both *about* and *for* Palestinian and Israeli-Jewish women. It explores the Israeli-Palestinian conflict from the perspectives of women activists, focusing primarily on the issues, strategies, and assumptions that women have used to address the interplay between the politics of gender and the politics of the Israeli-Palestinian conflict. In so doing, I sought to contribute to the project of documenting women's perspectives and struggles in the Middle East and to examine these struggles, offering some insights that Palestinian and Israeli-Jewish activists may find useful. At the same time, the book examines the ways in which the struggles of Palestinian and Israeli-Jewish women have been studied and presented both in the Middle East and in writing outside of the region.

The decision to discuss in the same book the struggles of Palestinian women in the West Bank and Gaza Strip and those of Jewish women peace activists in Israel was perhaps the most difficult decision I had to make, especially given my social location and identity as an Israeli-Jewish feminist. This is not yet another attempt by a liberal Israeli woman to impose her vision of women's liberation onto the multifaceted struggles of Palestinian women or to search for common ground between Palestinian and Israeli-Jewish women under the universalizing banner of global sisterhood at the expense of overlooking the unequal power relations that structure their relationship. Instead, I have sought to challenge throughout the book the presumed symmetry between Israelis and Palestinians, which is prevalent in most conventional accounts of the conflict.

All too often, media accounts and academic scholarship on the Israeli-Palestinian conflict have fallen into a trap of false symmetry. Typically, the Israeli-Palestinian conflict is presented as an intractable struggle between two parties over territory, identity, or security. What this interpretation overlooks is that the present phase of the conflict involves the Palestinians' struggle to rid themselves of the Israeli military occupation of the West Bank and Gaza Strip, which has not been benign. For Palestinians, the occupation has included, among other things, widespread arrests, detentions, curfews, and shootings, not to mention a maze of military laws and regulations that impose upon all aspects of daily life.[3] In spite of this, whenever there is an escalation in violence, the tendency has been to label Palestinians as the aggressors.

Such interpretations obscure the asymmetrical power relations between Palestinians and Israeli-Jews. One of the objectives of the simultaneous focus on the struggles of both Palestinian and Israeli-Jewish women is to stress the asymmetric nature of the Israeli-Palestinian conflict. This involves drawing attention to power relations, structured inequalities, and manifold differences between and among the Palestinian and Israeli-Jewish women's movements. More specifically, this entails pointing out how the history and politics of the Israeli-Palestinian conflict have differently situated Palestinian and Israeli-Jewish women in relation to gender issues, the struggle against the occupation, and one another.

This book covers six years, from the 1987 onset of the *intifada* to December 1993, including the aftermath of the September 1993 signing of the Declaration of Principles between the Israeli government and the Palestinian Liberation Organization (PLO). Yet, many of the questions, problems, and insights that shaped the conceptual underpinnings of this book have been informed, directly or indirectly, by the cumulative effects of my life experiences in Israel and in the United States and especially by my own political activism on the Israeli-

Palestinian conflict and involvement in struggles for peace, justice, and women's rights in the past twelve years.

Two major themes are woven throughout the book. The first involves the relationship between gender issues, women's resistance, and the history and politics of the Israeli-Palestinian conflict. The second involves the perspectives and struggles of Palestinian and Israeli-Jewish women activists. As a result, the book's scope is not limited to studying only the effects of the conflict on Palestinian and Israeli-Jewish women. Rather, it is grounded in the contention that the very peculiarities of gender relations both within and between Palestinian and Israeli communities have played a major role in shaping the conflict. Therefore, analyses of women's complex relations with men, and with masculinized political leaderships, and changes in prevailing conceptions of masculinity, femininity, and gender relations are viewed as crucial to the understanding of political developments such as the *intifada*, the November 1991 Madrid conference, the 1993 Declaration of Principles, or the Cairo agreement concerning the implementation of the Gaza and Jericho First plan, signed in 1994.

How do Palestinian and Israeli-Jewish women and groups address the connections between their struggles for gender equality and their resistance to the Israeli occupation of the West Bank and Gaza Strip? What are the changes that have taken place in dominant understandings of masculinity, femininity, and gender relations in both Palestinian and Israeli-Jewish communities, and how are these changes connected, if at all, to the historical trajectory of the Israeli-Palestinian conflict? These are some of the questions I seek to illuminate through a detailed exploration of such issues as the connections between the violence of the conflict and the escalation in violence against women, the relationship between militarism and sexism, the role of nationalism in the construction of individual and collective identities, and the prospects, pitfalls, and fragility of different forms of alliances between Israeli-Jewish and Palestinian women.

Following the introduction, the first two chapters of the book provide a broad historical and conceptual context for my exploration of the issues, strategies, and assumptions about gender and politics that shape the struggles of Palestinian and Israeli-Jewish women as well as the relationship between these two women's movements. Chapter 2 consists of theoretical exploration of the complex relationships between feminist frameworks, women's movements, and Middle East politics. The notion and methods of theorizing from women's lives and struggles are introduced and discussed in relation to contemporary feminist debates in the Middle East and more globally. In order to provide an alternative account of the Israeli-Palestinian conflict, we need to treat the daily experiences and struggles of Palestinian and Israeli-Jewish women as a particularly important location from which theories can emerge.

Contrary to conventional accounts of Middle East politics, which render women and gender issues invisible or unimportant, chapter 3 focuses on the interplay between gender and the Israeli-Palestinian conflict, surveying the implicit and explicit assumptions about masculinity, femininity, and gender relations that inform the politics and dominant interpretations of the Israeli-Palestinian conflict. The centrality of the conflict in the daily lives of Israelis and Palestinians made it perhaps the most significant catalyst for the consolidation of particular ideas about national identities and communities. The construction of Palestinian and Israeli-Jewish national identities, like that of any other national identities, has been shaped by particular understandings of gender roles and gender relations. This chapter examines the pivotal role of the Israeli discourse on national security and the Palestinian discourse on national liberation in shaping the terrain of understanding of both national identities and gender and setting the boundaries for women's resistance.

Chapter 4 outlines the history of Palestinian women's political mobilization from the turn of the century until the outbreak of the *intifada*. It examines the implications of particular turning points in the history of the Israeli-Palestinian conflict—such as the British Mandate, the 1936–39 Palestinian revolt, the 1948 war, which ended with the establishment of the state of Israel, and the 1967 Israeli occupation of the West Bank and Gaza Strip—on the lives and struggles of Palestinian women. Another significant turning point was the establishment of the Palestinian women's committees in 1978; these committees are affiliated with the major factions of the PLO and form the backbone of the organized Palestinian women's movement, often referred to as the "new" women's movement.

Following a detailed historical overview of the emergence of a distinct Palestinian women's movement in the West Bank and Gaza Strip, chapter 5 examines the political mobilization and involvement of Palestinian women since the beginning of the *intifada*. Although the women's committees were already active, the uprising induced significant changes in the scope, ideology, and strategies of women's struggles. The chapter pays particular attention to attempts by women to link their struggles for gender equality with their participation in the national struggle against the Israeli occupation of the West Bank and Gaza Strip. These connections have become more explicit with the establishment of new women's research, training, and counseling centers, by and for women, and with the emergence of local feminist discourses. The excitement that accompanied the crystallization of a feminist awareness within the Palestinian women's movement was interrupted by political developments such as the Gulf War, the Madrid conference and more recently the Declaration of Principles. The chapter examines the short- and long-term implications of these political developments for Palestinian women's lives and the various strategies they have utilized to confront these challenges.

Chapters 6 and 7 focus on the emergence and activities of the women's movement on the Israeli side of the Israeli-Palestinian divide. Beginning with the founding of the Women's Workers' Movement, in 1911—the first example of Jewish women's political organizing in Palestine—chapter 5 examines crucial turning points in the history of Jewish women activism until the *intifada*. These include the establishment of the state of Israel in 1948, the 1967 and 1973 wars, and the Israeli invasion of Lebanon in 1982, which served as a serious catalyst for the emergence of a distinct women's peace movement in Israel.

Chapter 7 examines the emergence of exclusively female and largely feminist peace groups founded during the first years of the *intifada*. The analysis highlights three groups in particular: Women in Black, the Women's Organizations for Women Political Prisoners (WOFPP), and Shani—Israeli Women Against the Occupation. The issues, assumptions, and strategies particular to women peace activists in Israel are analyzed in relation to the body of literature on women's peace activism in other parts of the world. The chapter also discusses Israeli women's attempts to articulate a feminist politics of peace, which links sexism and militarism and uses the theme of motherhood as a primary discourse of struggle against the militarization of society and of women's lives. The relationship between violence on the battlefield and the escalation of violence against women on the homefront, as well as different modes of women's organizing on these issues are carefully examined in this chapter.

Chapter 8 provides an overview of numerous grassroots initiatives designed to build bridges of trust, understanding, and collaboration between Jewish women in Israel and Palestinian women in the West Bank and Gaza Strip. These initiatives, largely triggered by the *intifada*, included demonstrations, mutual visits, dialogue groups, local and international conferences, and collaboration on particular projects such as those dealing with Palestinian prisoners' conditions and family reunification. Feminist scholars and activists from around the world who visited the region or read about these joint ventures in feminist magazines, have tended to treat these coalition-building attempts uncritically, presenting them as a proof that if Palestinian and Israeli women are able to build alliances transcending national boundaries, sisterhood is indeed global. Rather than idealize alliances between Palestinian and Israeli-Jewish women, I examine both their potential and pitfalls, stressing the need to recognize and confront structural differences in power and privilege that underlie the relationship between women across the Israeli-Palestinian divide.

The prospects for a just and lasting resolution of the Israeli-Palestinian conflict remain uncertain. What is quite clear, however, is that the contribution of Palestinian and Israeli-Jewish women to the peaceful resolution of the conflict continues to be ignored. Women, and their particular experiences and concerns, are rarely at the negotiation tables. For most media analysts, policymakers, and scholars of international politics, an international women's peace conference, or a joint demonstration in Jerusalem by Palestinian and Israeli-Jewish women, is no more than a human interest story. This book seeks to challenge such views. It treats the struggles of Palestinian and Israeli-Jewish women against the Israeli occupation, and for their own gender equality, as important political interventions. It further demonstrates how crucial the relationship between gender and politics is to understanding the Israeli-Palestinian conflict and the prospects for its resolution.

The lives and struggles of Palestinian and Israeli-Jewish women highlight dimensions of the Israeli-Palestinian conflict that often remain unaddressed in conventional accounts and scholarship on Middle East politics. They also offer alternative conceptualizations of peace and security and a clear vision for the transformation of the Middle East based on the principles of democracy and social justice. For peace in the Middle East to become more than an historical document and a famous handshake, peace initiatives must relate clearly to the lived realities of people and to the struggles of social movements to transform the region. As will become evident from both the history and contemporary struggles of the Palestinian and Israeli-Jewish women's movements, the rich experiences and political maturity of Palestinian and Israeli-Jewish women activists could make a real difference in the implementation of a just and lasting peace in the Middle East.

2

Feminist Theory, Gender Issues, and Middle East Politics

→ During a recent visit to Israel, in November 1993, following the signing of the Declaration of Principles between the Israeli government and the PLO, I was asked on several occasions for my opinion on what became known as the Oslo Accord. Given my familiarity with the cultural politics of Israel, where women are rarely asked for their views on current political events, I welcomed the opportunity to make some observations about the accord and to raise a number of questions about the hidden workings of gender and politics. Among the more general points I addressed were the exclusion of women from the negotiation table and how ironic it was that high-ranking Israeli generals, who spent a good portion of their lives waging war, have now become the ultimate voices of authority of peace while the perspectives and experience of women peace activists have been rendered trivial.

I was particularly eager to share my feminist perspective on the Oslo Accord, because I did notice some changes in the public political debate in Israel during that visit. For the first time it seemed that Israeli media and public relations campaigns had been recruited to mobilize support for peace rather than for war. In fact, more people than I had expected expressed open and unequivocal support for the agreement. At the same time, I soon came to realize that many things remained the same. Most men, regardless of their political positions on the Israeli-Palestinian conflict, resisted aspects of my interpretation that addressed gender issues such as the connection between the escalation

11

of the conflict and the increase in violence against women and grew absolutely impatient when I mentioned the word *feminism*. For most of them the term is still associated with images of men-hating radical bra-burners from the American 1960s, and their local followers, and thus has no relevance to political discussions about war and peace.

In Israel, as in other parts of the world, the term *feminism* triggers strong reactions from men as well as from many women with high stature and visibility, who either honestly or strategically disassociate themselves form feminism. Far from being popular, feminism in Israel is not considered a legitimate framework for political analysis, especially when the focus is on Middle East politics. Thus, even among politicians and activists, there have been (and still are) women who avoid identifying themselves or their activities as feminist. Despite unsympathetic-to-hostile public reactions, and a general atmosphere of backlash against feminism, women in Israel and around the world have increasingly aligned themselves with struggles for gender equality.

Feminism means different things to different people. Many powerful forces and preconceived notions of feminism and of struggles for gender equality have worked to undermine the importance of feminist movements and their perspectives on social and political life. This chapter explores the manifold interpretations, images, and practices associated with women's struggles and with the term *feminism* and examines the role of gender in the making of the Oslo Accord. It also establishes the importance of women's struggles as a location for theorizing about the relationship between gender and international politics and, more specifically, about the Israeli-Palestinian conflict and prospects for its resolution.

Women's Struggles and Feminist Theories

Women in varying sociocultural and political contexts have worked throughout history for the right to participate fully in the social, political, and economic life of their communities. Many did not regard themselves as feminists but the impetus for their mobilization and actions was in many ways similar to the impulses and motivations behind what we know as feminist struggles around the world. These struggles have been grounded in attempts to resolve the tensions and contradictions between what women want to be and do and what has been considered socially and politically acceptable, according to the written and unwritten rules within their societies or communities.

Women's struggles throughout history have taken different shapes and forms. Women have organized individually, collectively, and often alongside men, not only around gender and women's issues, but also for social and political transformation. In addition to the ongoing efforts to gain equal rights and to challenge gender discrimination, women have been at the forefront of peace and justice movements, environmental movements, and national liberation struggles.[1] Feminist theories emerged in the context of, and in direct relation to, these multifaceted struggles.

According to Chandra Mohanty, there is "an interdependent relationship between [feminist] theory, history, and struggle."[2] This interdependency is often reflected in the arguments and strategies of feminists, both scholars and activists. To come to terms with various forms of women's resistance, we need to make explicit the assumptions about gender, politics, and society that are central to a particular struggle and examine them in relation to the broader historical and sociopolitical context. A good place to start is to examine the transformations in the basic assumptions that have guided feminist theory in recent years.

Consider for example the demands of women of color, poor women, and lesbians for space and recognition within the international feminist movement, which came to the forefront during the United Nations Decade for Women (1975–85). These different groups of women called into question hegemonic understandings of feminism based on assumptions about the universality of women's experiences, which took as a model the daily lives, concerns, and priorities of heterosexual white upper-middle class women in Europe and North America.[3] Such critical interventions by women who felt marginalized and excluded within the movement forced many feminists to make explicit and question the basic assumptions that informed their understanding of feminism.

As a result, some of the taken for-granted assumptions about feminism have been challenged and transformed. Feminists have begun to recognize feminism as a contested term, whose understandings are shaped by different struggles, contexts, and social locations. Moreover, feminists have come to realize that the contested terrain of feminism is not marked only by gender lines but also by differences of race, class, ethnicity, nationality, culture, sexual orientation, political commitment, and theoretical framework. In other words, the prima facie assumption that sisterhood is global, or that the shared oppression of women around the world could provide the primary basis for solidarity among women, has been called into question.

What is the relevance of this discussion for understanding feminist projects and women's resistance in the Middle East, particularly in the context of the Israeli-Palestinian conflict? To answer this question, we should first make gender visible as an important dimension of the conflict. At the same time, we have to carefully examine the struggles of Israeli-Jewish and Palestinian women and capture the multiplicity of voices and perspectives within both movements. Of particular interest are the issues, strategies, and assumptions used by women to address the connections between gender and struggles against the Israeli occupation and toward a just resolution of the Israeli-Palestinian conflict.

Making Gender Visible

Before we make gender visible in the context of the Israeli-Palestinian conflict and point out how gender has and continues to significantly shape its various manifestations, we must be clear about what gender is. According to Jane Flax, gender is "a thought construct or category that helps us to make sense out of particular social worlds and histories, and . . . a social relation that enters into and partially constitutes all other social relations and activities."[4] In many cultures and societies, gender is often understood as interchangeable with sex, that is, the biological differences between males and females. In Hebrew, for instance, the terms *gender* and *sex* are indistinguishable. There is no specific word for gender. The word *min*, which translates as sex, is used to refer to both gender and sex. This conflation of "gender" with "sex" complicates feminist attempts to draw distinctions between the biological categories of male and female, the socially constructed notions of masculinity and femininity, and political positions based on masculinist or feminist assumptions.[5] Thus, many attempts by feminists to conceptualize gender begin with the assertion that gender does not rest primarily on biological sex differences but rather on various interpretations of behavior culturally associated with sex differences.[6]

The conceptualization of gender as a social, cultural, and political aspect of human existence and behavior enables the exploration of varieties of masculinity and femininity that are highly variable across cultures, time, and sociopolitical contexts. This understanding of gender takes into account the complex discourses, power relations, and practices that shape and inform particular notions of femininity, masculinity, and gender relations. In other words, taking gender seriously implies asking questions about a complex set of behaviors, social norms, systems of meaning, ways of thinking, and relationships that affect how we experience, understand, and represent ourselves as men and women.

From this perspective, we can see that gender is a fundamental element of social relations across cultures and time. Gender enables us to examine not only the relations between men and women, but also other social relations grounded in unequal relations of power and privilege. My apparent privileging of gender in this book is not based on an assumption that gender is more important than other dimensions of identity around which social relations are structured. Rather, it presumes that "gender intersects with racial, class, ethnic, sexual, and regional modalities of . . . identities."[7]

To come to terms with how gender works, both as a category of analysis and as a relational process that shapes the character and dominant representations of the Israeli-Palestinian conflict, let us first examine the United States sponsored peace process in the Middle East which was launched in Spring 1991, in the aftermath of the Gulf War. As we might expect, women and gender issues were excluded from the negotiations preceding the signing of the agreement, a fact which has remained for the most part unnoticed and unaddressed. What helps perpetuate and naturalize this exclusion from dominant accounts of the Israeli-Palestinian conflict is that certain understandings of masculinity, femininity, and gender relations that inform these accounts remain concealed, even when some prominent women who work in the spotlight gain recognition.

The November 1991 Madrid conference helped turn Hanan Mikhail-Ashrawi, the spokeswoman of the Palestinian delegation, into

1. The Palestinian negotiating team to the Middle East peace talks, Washington, D.C., July 1993. *Courtesy Shia Photo, Impact Visuals.*

a media celebrity. At the same time, instead of calling attention to the striking absence of more women at the negotiations, most accounts portrayed Dr. Ashrawi—who was not, in fact, present at the negotiation table—as a major figure, highlighting her intelligence, eloquence, Western dress and education.[8] Implicit in this representation was the assumption that talented, capable, Westernized women, who understand the political game and learn how to play it, can find a place and a voice in the arena of international politics. What most media accounts failed to recognize was that Hanan Ashrawi, like Zahira Kamal and Suad Ameri, the two other women in the Palestinian delegation, earned their places in the delegation as a result of the ongoing struggles of Palestinian women throughout the West Bank and Gaza Strip, especially since the outbreak of the *intifada*.[9] The massive political mobilization of Palestinian women and their explicit demands to take part in the

2. The Israeli negotiating team to the Middle East peace talks, Washington, D.C., July 1993. *Courtesy Shia Photo, Impact Visuals.*

decisions that affect their lives forced the Palestinian leadership to include women in social and political institutions. Nevertheless, women's access to decision-making remained limited.

As Cynthia Enloe argues, "the national political arena is dominated by men but allows women some select access."[10] In most cases, women who are able to enter or manage to "invade" that arena must be able to "successfully play at being men, or at least not shake masculine presumptions."[11] Unlike other prominent women leaders such as Margaret Thatcher, Indira Gandhi, Jeane Kirkpatrick and Golda Meir, who had previously gained recognition in the domain of world politics, the women in the Palestinian delegation did not act or talk like men. In fact, Hanan Ashrawi became a media celebrity, precisely because she introduced a fresh perspective and a nonmasculine voice to the arena of international politics.

3. Dr. Hanan Mikhail Ashrawi, former spokeswoman of the Palestinian delegation to the Middle East peace talks. *Courtesy Rick Reinhard, Impact Visuals.*

The popularity and success of the Palestinian spokeswoman was no doubt the major factor that prompted the appointment of women as spokespersons for the Syrian and Israeli delegations. Feminists, however, should celebrate these appointments with both caution and suspicion because they may indicate nothing more substantive than a contingent strategy of using women to sell international politics. It is still men who almost always decide when women's visibility or invisibility is likely to promote their national or international agendas. The gendered dimension of their decision-making remains, in most cases, concealed. As a result, the political efforts and accomplishments of many women have been relegated to the backstage of international politics.

Following the signing of the Oslo Accord, which led to the September 1993 Declaration of Principles, we had to read between the lines of the *New York Times* and the Israeli press to find out that two prominent Norwegian women played a pivotal role in the pre-negotiation stage that led to the signing of the Israeli-Palestinian agreement.[12] The first woman was Marianne Heiberg, a scholar at FAFO, the Norwegian Institute for Applied Social Science and author of a study of the living conditions in the Occupied Territories who also happened to be married to Johan Jorgen Holst, the Norwegian foreign minister, the person who received most of the credit for mediating the Oslo Accord. What remains largely unknown is that it was in fact Marianne Heiberg who introduced both the foreign minister (her husband) and Terje Rod Larsen, the executive director of FAFO (her boss), to the key people on the Israeli side. To achieve this goal, Heiberg used her personal and professional connections in Israel and in the West Bank and Gaza Strip, especially her close working relationship with Professor Yair Hirschfeld, who later became part of the Israeli team to the secret negotiations.[13]

The second prominent woman, whose role is even less known than Heiberg's was Mona Yoll, top advisor to the Norwegian foreign minister and married to FAFO's director, Terje Rod Larsen, whose role in orchestrating the Accord was widely recognized. There are few details about the exact role Mona Yoll played on the backstage of the secret negotiations in Oslo, but it is clear that she was instrumental in setting up the preliminary meetings leading to the direct secret negotiations and that she was present in most meetings. Her name and position, however, have been mentioned only in relation to her husband's, as evidence of the close connections between FAFO and the Norwegian government.[14]

The active roles of Marianne Heiberg and Mona Yoll in the pre-negotiation stage remain the best-kept secrets in the "his-tory" of the secret backstage negotiations that led to the Oslo Accord. The marginalization, or rather omission, of the contributions these two prominent women made to the peace process demonstrates how, in many instances, it is gender which determines who would be visible and who would remain invisible as well as whose work and services would get credit and whose would be taken for granted. This story confirms Enloe's argument that women's work in the arena of international politics, as in other domains, has been treated as if it were "natural" and thus taken for granted.[15] This gendered division of power and labor remains unnoticed in media coverage and "expert" analysis of the Israeli-Palestinian conflict.

There are a few obvious reasons that may account for the omission of gender as an important dimension of the Israeli-Palestinian conflict. First, according to commonsense understandings, gender is usually perceived as a synonym for women. Consequently, as are women, gender is excluded from most discussions concerning international politics. Second, according to conventional understandings, the practice of politics in general and of international politics in particular is associated with experiences, behavioral norms, meanings, and ways of thinking that are considered masculine and often negate or devalue concerns, interests, information, and meanings considered feminine.[16]

As Wendy Brown argues, "more than any other kind of human activity, *politics* has historically borne an explicitly masculine identity. It has been more exclusively limited to men than any other realm of endeavor and has been more intensely, self-consciously masculine than most other social practices."[17] As a result, any attempt to ask questions about gender in relation to international politics may appear threatening to men in that it makes them visible as men, and holds them accountable for the power and privilege they enjoy and take for granted. Moreover, making gender visible is also likely to be perceived as a threat to the social order and political status-quo locally and globally since they are grounded in and sustained by gendered divisions of power and labor.

If, indeed as Enloe insists, "making women invisible hides the working of both femininity and masculinity in international politics," then by making men visible as men we can expose the working of masculinity and femininity in world politics.[18] As a place to begin, consider for example the notions of masculinity, femininity, and gender relations implicit in the speech delivered by Israeli Prime Minister Yitzhak Rabin at the 1993 signing ceremony of the agreement between the Israeli government and the PLO.

Rabin's speech was filled with battlefield metaphors and a warrior's vocabulary, beginning on a personal note with an assertion that signing the agreement was not easy for him—"a soldier in Israel's war."[19] The speech provides numerous examples of what Carol Cohn called "the dominant voice of militarized masculinity and decontextualized rationality."[20] The language and images invoke very specific notions of masculinity and femininity: men are the fighters, the protectors who are ready to sacrifice their lives to protect women and children while women (and children) are the ever-present, passive victims in need of protection.[21] Images of "mothers [who] have wept for their sons," and "our children" and "our children's children" have been used throughout the speech to emphasize that the threat of "violence" and "terror" had to be met with militaristic and masculine actions of "defense" and "sacrifice."[22]

No political analyst or journalist commented on the gendered aspects of Rabin's speech; they were either unable to see those aspects or unwilling to consider them seriously. To treat gender as an important dimension of the Israeli-Palestinian conflict requires a different perspective on international politics, a perspective that can develop only if we look at the world through different lenses.

Why Gender-Sensitive Lenses?

The lenses we use determine not only what we look for and are able, or unable, to see, but also how we interpret these explorations. Making gender visible as an important dimension of social and political life requires gender-sensitive lenses.[23] In the context of Israeli-Palestinian conflict, gender-sensitive lenses, unlike conventional lenses, enable us to see how the conflict has been shaped by gendered assumptions, concepts, practices, and institutions.[24]

The gender-sensitive lenses I employ to examine the Israeli-Palestinian conflict are broad and multidimensional. They are designed

to capture interplays between gender and politics that transcend discussions of essential differences between women and men. Instead of
treating men and women as fixed categories grounded primarily in biological differences, this inquiry focuses on the social construction and
transformation of particular understandings of masculinity, femininity
and gender relations. Moreover, since the actual content of being a man
or a woman, and the rigidity of the categories themselves vary across
cultures and time, gender-sensitive lenses are context-specific. In other
words, they enable the exploration of changes in conceptions of masculinity, femininity, and gender relations throughout history and in
various sociocultural and political contexts.

Gender-sensitive lenses allow us to see the Israeli-Palestinian conflict both as a dynamic catalyst of and as a diversion from conflicts
around questions of identity and community *within* both the Palestinian and the Israeli-Jewish communities. In other words, the role of gender in the context of the Israeli-Palestinian conflict extends beyond
what it means to be a man or a woman; gender plays an
important role, shaping individual and collective identities as well
as dominant interpretations of the conflict and prospects for its
resolution.

Gender, Collective Identity, and Conflict

Media accounts and "expert" intepretations of the Israeli-
Palestinian Declaration of Principles presented the handshake between
Israeli Prime Minister Yitzhak Rabin and PLO Chairman Yasir Arafat
as the crossing of a significant border, both politically and psychologi-
cally. Yet, these rather simplistic interpretations reinforced the same
border they claimed to challenge: that between "us" and "them"—
Israeli-Jews and Palestinians. The excessive (often obsessive) focus on
the actual or symbolic significance of a handshake between official representatives of two national collectivities failed to acknowledge, and
indeed helped undermine, the ongoing struggles of women and other
progressive social movements in the Middle East within and across geo-
political borders.

Every invocation of the term *we* in the official text of the accord
and in the major speeches during the signing ceremony can be interpreted

4. The famous handshake: PLO chairman Yasir Arafat and Israeli Prime Minister Yizhak Rabin following the signing of the Declaration of Principles, Washington, D.C., September 13, 1993. *Courtesy Shia Photo, Impact Visuals*.

as an attempt to draw boundaries between those who are part of the community and those who are not, while at the same time erasing, or rendering invisible, boundaries *within* each community and bridges of understanding and solidarity that existed between citizens of both communities long before September 1993. Gender can be utilized to both mark and erase borders within and between communities. This is particularly evident in Rabin's speech where the word *we* appears more than twenty times. He describes the Israeli-Jewish collectivity through images that are both militaristic and masculinist:

We, the soldiers who have returned from battles stained with blood; we who have seen our relatives and friends killed before our eyes; we who have attended their funerals and cannot look in the eyes of their parents; we who have come from a land where parents bury their children; we who fought against you, the Palestinians (emphasis added).[25]

Rabin then defines Israeli-Jewish collectivity as an extended family and asserts his role as one of its patriarchs:

We have come from a people, a home, a family that has not known a single year, nor a single month, in *which mothers have not wept for their sons*. We have come to try and put an end to the *hostilities* so that our children, our children's children, will no longer experience *the painful cost of war: violence and terror*. We have come *to secure* their lives...(emphasis added).[26]

Rabin's use of the term *we* is grounded in a particular understanding of gender and gender relations, in which Israeli collectivity depends upon men who are ready to fight and die on the battlefield and upon women who fulfill their duties as "mothers of the nation," not only as caretakers and keepers of the homefront, but also as suppliers of children to the nation.[27] Rabin's speech reveals his inability to imagine a Jewish-Israeli collectivity that does not depend on the persistence of the Israeli-Palestinian conflict and on the preservation of traditional conceptions of masculinity, femininity, and gender relations.

Gender-sensitive lenses may illuminate the processes and practices that enabled governments in the Middle East to use the Arab-Israeli conflict, especially its Israeli-Palestinian dimension, to justify both the neglect and marginalization of other social issues and discriminatory state policies against disenfranchised groups such as women and minorities. In addition, these lenses will help us focus our attention on attempts by individuals and groups to address the interplays between gender and politics and transform dominant conceptions of masculinity, femininity, and gender relations by introducing alternative possibilities and practices. A close look at the lives and struggles of women activists on both sides of Palestinian-Israeli divide is necessary in order to come to terms with the role of gender in shaping and transforming conventional understandings of the Israeli-Palestinian conflict.

Theorizing from Women's Struggles[28]

The perspectives of Palestinian and Israeli-Jewish women on gender relations and on the Israeli-Palestinian conflict, and the struggles they have waged on these issues are informed by certain assumptions about gender and politics. These perspectives evolve and tend to change over time in relation to women's daily experiences and struggles, particular problems that confront them, and the broader sociocultural and political context that shapes their priorities. They provide women with a sense of direction and purpose as well as with general frameworks and theories of struggle that enable them to make sense of and cope with challenges they face in their daily lives.[28]

One major objective of this book is not only to make explicit the frameworks and strategies that underlie the struggles of Palestinian and Israeli women but also to demonstrate their relevance and contribution to the development of feminist theory, research, and practice and more particularly, to the exploration of women's struggles in other parts of the world. Instead of introducing one particular theoretical framework to be later applied to the Israeli-Palestinian conflict, I treat the daily experiences and struggles of Palestinian and Israeli women activists as locations where theorizing takes place. In other words, Palestinian and Israeli women activists are treated as social and political theorists.

To write about women activists as theorists is to de-marginalize their experiences and to stress their political agency. But it is also to recognize that agency is shaped by a particular context of power relations. It requires us not only to record women's voices or perspectives, but also to establish their authority and expertise in a domain of engagement—the political arena—and on a particular topic—the Israeli-Palestinian conflict—from which women's perspectives and gender issues have been previously excluded.

In the context of the Israeli-Palestinian conflict, theorizing from women's struggles is an attempt to elicit alternative interpretations of the conflict. According to Chandra Mohanty, such a project entails "the very practice of remembering against the grain of 'public' or hegemonic history, [and] of locating the silences and the struggle to assert knowledge which is outside the parameters of the dominant."[29] Particularly relevant to this discussion is a new genre of feminist scholarship that views women's life experiences and struggles as valuable locations from which critical analyses and theorizing about and for women should begin.[30]

Whether we are aware of it or not, theorizing is part of our daily lives; we ask questions, make assumptions, gather relevant information, and draw conclusions. Theorizing about daily experiences and struggles has been an integral part of the emergence and development of social movements in general and women's movements in particular. The assumptions, issues, and strategies that inform a particular struggle constitute a theoretical framework; they are the lenses through which we interpret the world. Contrary to common views, the crystallization of theories does not occur only in academic settings. There are theories which evolve in direct relation to particular struggles.

Feminist theories, for example, emerged in the context of women's struggles around the world while Marxist theories have their grounding in the rich histories of labor movements. These theories, however, like the movements that inspired them, should be discussed in relation to a particular sociocultural and political context. That is, the struggles of women in the West Bank and Gaza Strip and in Israel need to be explored, on one hand, in relation to feminist theorizing and women's struggles worldwide, and on the other, in relation to Middle East politics and to women's political activism throughout the region.

Women's Struggles and Middle East Politics

Recent scholarship on women in the Middle East, including biographies, oral histories, testimonies, poetry, and research, highlights previously unknown accounts of women's lives and struggles in the region.[31] These accounts point out that women in the Middle East have raised the issues of women's rights and gender inequalities since the turn of the century through the publication of books and the establishment of magazines and special forums explicitly advocating the improvement of women's lives.[32] This growing body of literature by and about women in the Middle East calls attention to the range of activities and multiplicity of voices and perspectives among women in the region.

Middle East "experts," however, often fail to display this diversity and instead tend to reinforce stereotypical images. As Orayb Najjar asserts "somewhere out there in the land of Middle East Studies live

'Arab-Muslim-Middle-Eastern women'. As a Muslim Arab who has lived in the Middle East, I do not know the women about whom most Middle East 'experts' write."[33] To challenge the stereotypical depictions of Middle Eastern women, Najjar makes an effort to include in her book "women of different ages who have lived through various periods of Palestinian history (British, Jordanian, Israeli, and intifada) and women with different kinds of experiences and educational levels . . . illiterate women, educated women, some who are deeply involved in the struggle against the Israeli occupation, as well as others who are merely struggling to get by or get an education."[34]

Another example of a project that challenges the stereotypical depictions of Middle Eastern women is Arlene Elowe Macleod's detailed exploration of the practice of veiling among lower-middle-class women in Cairo.[35] MacLeod notes that "the veil has been an obsession of Western writers from early travelogues to more recent television docudramas, serving as the symbol par excellence of women as oppressed in the Middle East, an image that ignores indigenous cultural constructions of the veil's meanings and reduces a complex and everchanging symbolism into an ahistorical reification."[36] To counter this image, MacLeod shows how the meaning of any act of veiling depends upon its context. There is no single reason why women veil, and in some cases women may veil as a sign if their own agency.[37]

The stereotypical image of Middle Eastern women as veiled, voiceless, and powerless victims contributes to the backlash against women's movements and feminist projects in the Middle East; it renders invisible more than a century of women's struggles in the region and silences the multiple voices and perspectives on gender, culture, and politics that have been articulated by these women. Consider for example a recent front-page article in the New York Times titled "Fundamentalists Impose Culture on Egypt," which was accompanied by a photo of veiled Egyptian women and girls.[38] The article itself did not only fail to discuss the relationship between gender, Islam, Egyptian politics, and international politics, it failed altogether to mention women. Yet, the visual message was clear and explicit: women were the victims of a relentless fundamentalist campaign and the traditional Islamic dress served as a symbol of the "strict Islamic culture" they seek to impose.[39]

Such images of Middle Eastern women are often contrasted with those of liberated Western women. This juxtaposition rests on a notion of essential differences *between* women in the Middle East and women in Europe and North America on one hand and on the erasure of difference *within* each group of women on the other, a point of view that has come to be known and criticized as "orientalism."[40] In addition to rendering women powerless and voiceless, and erasing diversity, orientalist representations contribute to the backlash against Western women by creating the illusion that gender equality and women's liberation have already been achieved in Western countries.

The stereotypical depictions of Middle Eastern women have served another purpose. The reinforced otherness of Middle Eastern women has also served as pretext or justification for Western intervention in the Middle East. During the Iranian revolution of 1979, the Western media utilized images of veiled Iranian women in order to mobilize public opinion in the United States and in Europe in support of continued U.S. intervention in Iranian politics as well as in other parts of the region. The veil was invoked as a symbol of Islamic repression, a supposition that ignores the fact that many highly educated women took up the veil voluntarily, as a symbol of struggle and of their opposition to the Shah.[41] According to Cynthia Enloe, a similar subtext was used during the Gulf crisis and war: "by contrasting the allegedly liberated US woman tank mechanic with the Saudi woman deprived of a driver's license, U.S. reporters are implying that the United States is the advanced civilized country whose duty is to take the lead in resolving the Persian Gulf crisis."[42]

A critical examination of stereotypical depictions of Middle Eastern women and the political ends they have served must be an integral part of any discussion of feminist projects and women's resistance in the context of the Israeli-Palestinian conflict. One way of doing this is by providing detailed accounts of particular women's struggles in the region and by highlighting the differences that exist among Middle Eastern women. In addition, we must examine the different discourses about gender equality and women's liberation that have informed women's resistance in the Middle East in relation to feminist theories and discourses about gender, politics, and society in other contexts. As Deniz Kandiyoti points out, women's struggles and feminist projects in the region ought to be treated as "both intensely local, grappling with their own histories and specificities, and international, in that they have been in dialogue, both collaborative and adversarial, with broader currents of thought and activism."[43]

Scholarly work on women's resistance, gender issues, and feminism in the Middle East reflects multiple perspectives and different emphases. Recent writings have focused primarily on women activists themselves, stressing their political agency and challenging their passive portrayals.[44] Representative of this genre is Badran's and Cooke's recent anthology, documenting a century of Arab feminist writing. They employ a working definition of feminism that "involves one or more of the following: an awareness by women that as women they are systematically placed in a disadvantaged position; some form of rejection of enforced behaviors and thought; and attempts to interpret their own experiences and then to improve their position or lives as women."[45] Based on this broad definition, they classify writings by Arab women to these three rubrics: Awareness, Rejection, and Activism.[46]

Another trend has been to explore the evolution of women's resistance through time and in relation to the changing sociopolitical conditions in the region, that is, to rewrite the history of the region based on women's perspectives and experiences.[47] More recently women's lives and struggles in the Middle East have been examined in relation to a variety of social issues, institutions, and movements. This perspective is reflected in the outpouring of literature on such issues as the relationship between gender issues and nationalism, Islam, development or democracy.[48]

These approaches to the study of women in the Middle East are not mutually exclusive but rather complimentary. Each approach reflects a crucial dimension of women's struggles. Yet, taken separately, they are often unable to capture tensions and complexity or reflect the multiplicity of voices among women. Since women are not a monolithic group, any single framework will not be sufficient to capture the complexity and the different dimensions and particularities of their struggles. In other words, we need to move beyond typologies and into the complex realms and locations where women actually make history and theory.[49]

Conceptual frameworks that seek to account for the relationship between gender and the politics of the Israeli-Palestinian conflict and to theorize about women's resistance in this context cannot emerge in academic settings and then be applied to case studies dealing with the Israeli-Palestinian conflict. Theorizing on these issues has to emerge from the complex and multidimensional daily struggles of Palestinian and Israeli women whose lives have been entangled in the conflict and whose stories and attempts to draw connections between gender and politics have been largely ignored in conventional accounts.

Against the background of the conventional interpretations of the Israeli-Palestinian conflict, the following chapter will focus on the daily experiences of Palestinian and Israeli-Jewish women. By examining the evolution of theories and strategies that link gender issues with politics, and by looking at the Israeli-Palestinian conflict from the perspectives of both Palestinian and Israeli-Jewish women, the chapter calls attention to crucial dimensions of the Israeli-Palestinian conflict that have heretofore tended to remain unexplored.

3

Nationalisms, Gender, and the Israeli-Palestinian Conflict

➥ Picture an op-ed piece titled "Gender and the Israeli-Palestinian Conflict," in the Sunday edition of the *New York Times* or a special edition of CNN's World News featuring interviews with Palestinian and Israeli women activists on the gendered dimensions of the September 1993 Declaration of Principles and its implications for women's lives and struggles in the region. These would be hard to imagine because the Israeli-Palestinian conflict is analyzed and discussed as if it were ungendered. The fact that the conflict is distinctly shaped by and has significantly shaped gender relations and certain understandings of femininity and masculinity has not been an issue for serious political concern. It is the aim of this chapter to show that this view is mistaken.

Gender, like other such structures of social identity as culture, race, ethnicity, class, sexuality, and nationality, shapes who we are, what we have, and how we make sense of the social and political world. Taking gender seriously, therefore, involves asking questions about the social construction of individual and collective identities as well as about daily practices that reflect often taken-for-granted distinctions between what it means to be a man or a woman.

In the context of the Israeli-Palestinian conflict taking gender seriously involves addressing such questions as how are particular understandings of masculinity, femininity, and gender relations shaped and transformed in relation to the historical trajectory of the Israeli-Palestinian conflict? What sort of transformations in assumptions about

31

gender identities and relationships between women and men may contribute to the peaceful resolution of the conflict? And what have been the contributions of the Palestinian and Israeli-Jewish women's movements to this process? These questions necessitate a critical discussion about the modalities of masculinity and femininity that underlie dominant practices and interpretations of the Israeli-Palestinian conflict, and more broadly, about the role of gender in both the construction and the consolidation of Palestinian and Israeli-Jewish national identities.

Gender and the Boundaries of Nationalism

It would be an understatement to say that the Israeli-Palestinian conflict has shaped the lives of at least three generations of Israelis and Palestinians. The Arab-Israeli conflict, particularly its Israeli-Palestinian dimension, has played a central role not only in the daily lives of people throughout the Middle East but also in the lives of Palestinians and Jews living outside the physical land of Israel and the Occupied Territories, many of whom see their existence as inseparable from political developments in the region. The Israeli-Palestinian conflict has served both as the catalyst and the touchstone for the consolidation of particular notions of national "imagined community" for Palestinians and for Israeli-Jews respectively.[1]

For Palestinians, the imagined community came to be seen as a future sovereign Palestinian state. Apart from differences concerning the territorial boundaries and the political and social character of their future state, there is a broad consensus among Palestinians that the principles of national self-determination and territorial sovereignty are inseparable and crucial to the survival of the Palestinian people. A consensus around the same principles has served as the basis for the Israeli-Jewish imagined community. Yet, while Jews realized their dream and established a Jewish state, this has come at the expense of Palestinians, whose desire to fuse national self-determination with territorial sovereignty remains unfulfilled. This turn of events has in many ways formed the basis for the present conflict.

The insistence on the inseparability of national self-determination and territorial sovereignty has reinforced a sharp distinction between "us" and "them" that has its origins in the early conflicts between

Zionist settlers and the indigenous Palestinians population and has been reinforced by the efficacy of the Israeli-Palestinian conflict. The centrality of the Israeli-Palestinian conflict in the daily lives and practices of Israelis and Palestinians since that time has helped generate the answers to the question "who we are," that played such an important role in shaping Palestinian and Israeli-Jewish collectivities.

One set of answers to this question that has its origins in the rigid distinction between "us" and "them" has structured the relationship between Palestinians and Israeli-Jews. But an overemphasis on this distinction often overlooks differences within each community and thus other possible answers to the question "who are we." Just as Palestinians and Israeli-Jews have articulated different, and often competing answers to this question, there have been multiple answers within each national collectivity. These answers always involve, explicitly or implicitly, particular assumptions about masculinity, femininity, and gender relations.

Deniz Kandiyoti points out that these answers "are not given, but fought over and contested by political actors whose definitions of *who* and *what* constitutes that nation have a crucial bearing on notions of national unity and alternative claims to sovereignty as well as on the sorts of gender relations that should inform the nationalist project."[2] Competing definitions of who and what constitutes the imagined community often reflect differences in social location, experience, and power. In other words, as Cynthia Enloe points out "women and men . . . struggle with each other over whose experiences—of humiliation, of insecurity, of solidarity—will define the community in its new national manifestation."[3]

At times, women win small victories but, for the most part, it is men who set the agenda of nationalist projects. This is not always clear from the outset because nationalism in its different forms offers a vision that speaks to women by providing them with a community in which they can be members and with incentives to become political actors. According to Enloe, "national consciousness has induced many women to feel confident enough to take part in public organizing and public debate," because more than other ideologies, nationalism "has a vision that includes women."[4]

The problem, however, is that, women often do not have a say in determining the terms of their inclusion in nationalist projects, especially when they unfold in a militarized context like that of the Israeli-Palestinian conflict. In highly militarized societies, women's participation in and contribution to their national collectivities often result in the militarization of their lives both as individuals and as members of the community. The following examples demonstrate how national movements have been able to mobilize women's identities, social roles, and bodies by militarizing particular notions of femininity on the one hand and by reinforcing the power and privilege of a militarized masculinity on the other.

In the early 1950s, Israel's first prime minister David Ben-Gurion, turned the issue of women's fertility into a national priority, arguing that "increasing the Jewish birthrate is a vital need for the existence of Israel, and [that] a Jewish woman who does not bring at least four children into the world is defrauding the Jewish mission."[5] Based on these convictions, Ben-Gurion initiated a special state fund designed to pass out symbolic money rewards to "heroine mothers"—women who had ten children or more.[6]

In the 1980s, this "necessity" was once again invoked to fit the political agenda of the time. The newly formed "Efrat Committee for the Encouragement of Higher Birth Rates" linked the public debate on abortion at the time to the widely disseminated worry among Israelis that Israel's survival depended on its victory over Palestinians in what they saw as a demographic war. Utilizing the rhetoric of religious anti-abortion groups and the memory of the Holocaust, the Efrat Committee called upon Jewish women to fulfill their national duty by bearing more children to replace the Jewish children killed by the Nazis during the Holocaust. In addition, then advisor to the minister of health, Haim Sadan, proposed to force every Jewish woman considering an abortion to watch a slide show that included along with grotesque slides of dead fetuses in rubbish bins, pictures of dead Jewish children in the Nazi concentration camps.[7] This proposal was narrowly defeated, but its message was clear: abortion was an act of national treason while bearing more children turned Israeli-Jewish mothers into national heroines.

Attempts to promote the virtues of heroine mothers have been prevalent in many national movements because along with praising women's participation in the national struggle, they reinforce a certain understanding of femininity and womanhood grounded in women's

5. A Palestinian woman trying to prevent Israeli soldiers from arresting her son, Occupied East Jerusalem, 1989. *Courtesy John Toradi, Impact Visuals.*

reproductive role and nurturing capabilities. In the Palestinian context, for example, the tendency to depict women as "mothers of the nation," which gained particular importance during the first three years of the *intifada*, embodied both the steadfastness and cultural continuity associated with Palestinian national liberation and the warmth, care, and compassion associated with womanhood. As Nahla Abdo points out "the construction of motherhood equals nationhood within the Palestinian context emerged as an expression of Palestinian lived reality. Expulsion from the homeland and refugeeism in foreign territories provided the impetus for the mother-nation relationship."[8]

Despite significant differences in context, women in both the Palestinian and Israeli cases were encouraged to participate in nationalist projects but were publicly praised only when they participated as women. In other words, to fulfill their national duty women had to accept primary responsibility for reproduction and cultural transmission of their respective communities. The "mothers of the nation" have nonetheless often been relegated to the margins of their collectivities. Despite this, the intensity of the Israeli-Palestinian conflict and its centrality in people's everyday lives have naturalized the tendency to overlook differences within one's imagined community, particularly the narrow roles allotted to women, and tamed, until recently, possible resistance on the part of women.

National Security and National Liberation

The intensity of the Israeli-Palestinian conflict and its significant military component over the years has contributed to the consolidation of Israeli-Jewish collectivity through an emphasis on its national security. For Palestinians, on the other hand, national liberation has emerged as the most important focus of their collective identity, especially following the Israeli occupation of the West Bank and Gaza Strip in 1967 and the emergence of the PLO as a vehicle of national aspirations. Within the Israeli-Jewish society, the constant invocations of Israel's security concerns has helped reinforce an overt and covert militarization of peoples' lives. For Palestinians, on the other hand, the centrality of the conflict has manifested itself in the privileging of national liberation not only as the primary ideology of struggle against Israeli occupation but also as a principle discourse that shapes certain ideas and ways of thinking about Palestinian identity and community.

National security and national liberation discourses are similar in that they view the potency and unity of the nation as superior to issues raised by private citizens and various social groups within that nation. As a result of the primary emphases on national security and national liberation respectively, different social and economic problems within both communities have been rendered less important and thus put on the backburners until the Israeli-Palestinian conflict would be resolved.

Still, the differences between Israeli-Jewish and Palestinian nationalisms, which are often overlooked, are far greater than the similarities. They are based on fundamental differences in the history and social context of the two national movements, and most particularly, in the striking disparities of power and privilege between them. On the one hand is the difference between institutionalized state nationalism

6. An occasional "encounter" between Israeli and Palestinian men: Israeli soldiers round up Palestinian men, Occupied East Jerusalem, March 1991. *Courtesy Francisco Conde, Impact Visuals.*

and the nationalism of a liberation movement, and on the other the disparities in power relations between an occupying state and a population struggling to rid itself of that state's rule.[9] The distinction between Israel's discourse of national security and Palestinian discourses of national liberation are both theoretically necessary and politically important.

As has been suggested throughout this discussion, the discourses of national security and national liberation, like most nationalist discourses, involve explicit or implicit assumptions about masculinity, femininity, and gender relations. For example, both discourses affirm the centrality of territorial sovereignty for the preservation of their national collectivities. Consequently, men in both communities are socialized to be the protectors and liberators of their nations—that is, to seek to either maintain control or gain control over land. Women, on the other hand, are cast as those whose role is to reproduce the nation and are, therefore, in need of protection. This gendered division of labor and power reinforces the tendency to represent the nation and its territory as a woman to be protected, or in some cases occupied. Representations of nation-as-woman are common in almost all nationalist discourses and are quite often highly sexualized: "whenever the power of the nation is invoked—whether it be in the media, in scholarly texts, or in every day conversation—we are more likely than not to find it couched as a *love of country*: an eroticized nationalism."[10]

A careful examination of the Hebrew language and of a number of taken-for-granted practices easily demonstrates how central the theme of nation-as-woman has been to the construction of Israeli-Jewish nationalism. The Hebrew word *kibush*, which is the most commonly used term for the Israeli occupation of the West Bank and Gaza Strip, is also used to describe conquest either of a military target or of a woman's heart. This conflation of women and military targets is not merely linguistic; it informs numerous practices in Israeli society, most particularly in the military. During military training exercises, for example, strategic targets are often named after significant women in the soldiers' lives. This common practice implies that women, like military targets, must be protected so that they will not be conquered or controlled by the enemy.

Interpretations and appropriations of the relationship between women and their national collectivities vary across sociocultural contexts. These interpretations are not stable but rather change over time and in relation to broader political developments. The *intifada*, for example, gave rise to dramatic transformations in conventional notions of femininity, masculinity and gender relations in Palestinian society. The massive political mobilization of women in the West Bank and Gaza Strip called into question passive images of women as dutiful, daughterly, maternal, and chaste.

The new political reality created an atmosphere in which some prevailing attitudes about the sanctity of the woman's body became the topics of public discussions and contestation.[11] Nahla Abdo, for example, writes about *Um al-Asirah*, the mother of a Palestinian woman imprisoned during the *intifada*, who was one of the keynote speakers at the 1990 annual convention of the Union of Palestinian Women's Associations in North America (UPWA).[12] Taking pride in her daughter's imprisonment, *Um al-Asirah* asserted that even if her daughter will be sexually harassed or raped in jail, this will not deter her or any other Palestinian woman from political activism.[13] In addition, Abdo describes other significant changes such as public discussions on the subject of political rape that took place in a number of villages, stressing the fact that women raped or sexually assaulted by Israeli soldiers and police were not considered outcasts any more.[14]

Changes in social attitudes towards political rape within Palestinian society were triggered and facilitated by the dynamic nationalism the *intifada* sparked. As mentioned, issues such as sexual abuse and rape of Palestinian women prisoners in Israeli jails, which were rarely discussed in public prior to the *intifada* because they were considered socially taboo, were being discussed in the open during the first three years of the uprising. In order to encourage Palestinian women to remain politically active at the forefront of the *intifada*, it was necessary to treat sexual assault and rape as no different than other forms of torture.

Despite the undeniable change in social attitudes toward Palestinian women prisoners, women's bodies remain central to the Palestinian national project. The treatment of Palestinian women's prisoners who survived rape and sexual violence in the Israeli jails as national heroines instead of as outcasts, does not challenge but rather helps reinforce the centrality of women's bodies in Palestinian national discourse. The nation is still depicted as a woman's body whose violation by the enemy forces its men to rush to her defense.

Palestinian women's identities and bodies have in fact become the battlefields for both types of nationalisms: Israeli national security on one hand and Palestinian national liberation on the other. Palestinian women embodied Palestine not only for Palestinians but also for their Israeli occupiers.[15] The Israeli military has used the discourse of national security to justify the massive arrests of Palestinian women and their forceful interrogation. Threats and actual sexual assaults were used during interrogations to pressure women to get incriminating evidence against family members and force the families to turn Palestinian fugitives to the Israeli authorities, as well as to deter women from resisting the occupation. To counter such practices and fight back, proud Palestinian nationalists, men and women, have sent a loud and clear message to the Israeli occupation authorities that is best summed up in *Um al-Asirah*'s assertion: "I know that my daughter might be sexually harassed or even raped, but your threats will not deter her or other women from political activism."[16]

Gender and National Security

Marcia Freedman, perhaps the first outspoken feminist in the Israeli Parliament (Knesset), describes Israel as "a country where the liberation of women . . . [is] seen as a threat to national security."[17] According to Freedman, this perception is a clear indication of the special role of gender within the social and political fabric of Israeli society, as well as of the centrality of national security to defining the contours of Israeli-Jewish collective identity. In Israel, national security is the principle discourse to which political discussion and practice must refer in order to be taken seriously. However, there is no given or objective definition of security in any society, including Israel; its meanings depend first and foremost on how a nation defines itself because this definition often shapes the understandings of security.[18]

The processes and practices that gave rise to the dominant interpretations of "national security" in Israel, and to the centrality of this discourse, are complex and have changed over time. Nevertheless, these interpretations have always been gendered. In the name of national security, certain meanings of masculinity and femininity have been deployed to consolidate the Israeli-Jewish state and society. Political practices and rhetoric that stressed the need to create a united front against the enemy have reinforced the central role of national security discourse in shaping Israeli's understandings of identity and community.

Through consistent references to the survival of Israel and of the Jewish people as a whole, particular conceptions of national security have become hegemonic in Israel. Drawn from different strands of Zionist ideology and selective interpretations of Jewish history and the Arab-Israeli conflict, these conceptions rest on particular assumptions about masculinity, femininity, and gender relations. The construction of an Israeli nationality has been significantly shaped by the assertion of an aggressive and highly militarized masculinity, justified by the need to end a history of weakness and suffering. Images of Israeli-Jewish men who are exceedingly masculine—that is, pragmatic, protective, assertive and emotionally tough—have been contrasted with a fairly traditional notion of femininity on the one hand, and with images of the helpless and powerless Jew in the diaspora on the other.

The practice of calling those born in Israel *sabras* stands as an exemplary metaphor for this reassertion of masculinity. Named after the indigenous cactus fruit, which is tough and prickly on the outside and soft and sweet on the inside, the *sabra* motif has played an important role in the socialization of a new generation of Jewish men born in Israel. These "new" men have been portrayed as the antithesis of the weak, persecuted Jews, most commonly associated with the collective traumatic memories of the Holocaust.[19]

In addition to the negative juxtaposition of the Israeli-born Jew with women and with Jews in the diaspora, the *sabra* has been contrasted with images of the so-called enemy. These various juxtapositions resemble the general pattern of self-other cartographies of identity. In this particular context, the "self," represented by the *sabra* image, marks the center of Israeli collectivity, while the "other," or more correctly the "others," serve as its contrasts. In other words, Jews who were not born in Israel or do not live there, women, and Arabs (especially Palestinians)—all characterized as non-masculine—are presented as potential threats to the *sabra's* identity. Against this background, the *sabra* man is encouraged to come to terms with and assert his masculine identity. And, the primary responsibility for the construction and validation of Israeli men's identities lies in the hands of the Israeli military.

Gender and the Militarization of People's Lives

Perhaps the most significant implication of the centrality of national security within Israeli society is that the army has become the most important institution in Israeli society; the gradual militarization of people's lives has followed closely behind. According to Enloe, the process of militarization which is always gendered, intensifies "when a community's politicized sense of its own identity becomes threaded through with pressures for its men to take up arms, [and] for its women to loyally support brothers, husbands, sons and lovers to become soldiers."[20] Yet Enloe insists that "militarization is a process that is not geared with natural inclinations and easy choices. It usually involves confusion and mixed messages. On one hand, it requires the participation of women as well as men. On the other hand, it is a social construction that usually privileges masculinity."[21]

This privileging of masculinity is quite evident in Israel. To be a man implies first and foremost being a soldier. Israeli-Jewish men are

7. A cactus, the symbol of the Israeli Sabra who is characterized as tough on the outside and tender on the inside. From "Tough and Tender," an art installation by Gabi Gofbarg. *Courtesy Gabi Gofbarg, 1992.*

The native-born Israeli has been given the sobriquet "sabra," after the wild cactus which flourishes in the arid soil of Israel. The fruit of this plant is prickly on the outside and soft on the inside. This implies that our sabras are tough, brusque, inaccessible, and yet surprisingly gentle and sweet within. The nickname is given affectionately and is borne with pride by our young, who enjoy the reputation that they cannot be "savored" from outward appearances.

"But you don't look Jewish!" is the dubious compliment a young Israeli usually receives when he goes abroad. The sabra is generally a head taller than his father, often blond and freckled, often blue-eyed and snub-nosed. He is cocky, robustly built, and likes to walk in open sandals in a free-swinging, lazy slouch. He speaks Hebrew either in a rapid-

8. The Israeli *Sabra*. From "Tough and Tender," an art installation by Gabi Gofbarg. *Courtesy Gabi Gofbarg, 1992.*

required to complete a three-year mandatory military service; after that they serve in the reserves and complete at least one month of military service a year until they are fifty-five years old. Military service constitutes a necessary rite-of-passage, for a man to earn his place in Israeli society and to be considered a loyal citizen. As was mentioned earlier, the militarized masculinity of Israeli-Jewish men is associated with personal qualities such as pragmatism, assertiveness, emotional toughness, and readiness to sacrifice one's life for the homeland. This notion of masculinity has been shaped and reinforced by the constant background of the Arab-Israeli conflict. In this context, the exploration of alternative, non-militarized forms of masculinity, which very few Israeli-Jewish men explicitly undertake, is often perceived as an act of national treason.

While Israeli-Jewish men learn to fight and protect, women are socialized to be caretakers on one hand and deferential and in need of protection on the other. The intensity of the Israeli-Palestinian conflict has contributed to the fact that Israeli women's identities are often defined in relation to significant men in their lives. As former member of parliament Geula Cohen, founder of the extremist right-wing Tehiya party, asserted "the Israeli woman is a wife and a mother in Israel, and therefore it is *her nature* to be a soldier, a wife of a soldier, a sister of a soldier. This is her reserve duty. She is continually in military service" (emphasis added).[22] The militarization of women's roles in Israel implies that women who do not comply with their assigned duties are viewed not only as rejecting their personal responsibilities but, even worse, as refusing to contribute their share as members of the Israeli collectivity.

In addition to their socially-assigned responsibilities as keepers of the homefront, Israeli-Jewish women have to serve in the military. Israel was the first, and is still one of the few states in which women are recruited to serve in the army through a national recruitment law.[23] This law fueled a prevailing myth regarding gender equality in Israel. Images of attractive, exotic, young Israeli women in military uniform with machine guns slung over their shoulders have been systematically deployed in Israeli public relations campaigns to emphasize the seriousness of the continual threat to Israel's national security and the extent to which the nation is prepared to sacrifice to meet this threat. Although within Israeli society the separation of masculine and feminine domains has preserved men's roles as protectors and women's as needing protection, to the world, the state of Israel has portrayed the

9. An Israeli woman soldier posing for a photo taken by foreign reporters. Women's Training Camp, Israel, April 1991. *Courtesy Henrik Saxgren/2 maj, Impact Visuals.*

seriousness of the conflict by emphasizing that even women are fighting. Contrary to liberal feminist interpretations, the recruitment of Israeli women into the military has not been presented as a principle grounded in a struggle for gender equality, but rather as an inevitable necessity.

In sharp contrast to the popular image of the Israeli woman soldier, official accounts reveal that at least seventy percent of the Israeli women who serve in the military are trained to occupy traditional women's roles. Most spend their two-year service as clerk-typists, folding parachutes, working in base kitchens, or serving entertainment troops. The remainder are loaned out to various government ministries to cover shortages; they work as teachers, policewomen, nurse's aides, and so forth.[24] The military's practice of loaning women to civil service institutions blurs the distinctions between battlefield and homefront and reinforces the centrality of the Israeli military in all spheres of Israeli society.

Women serving in the Israeli military belong to the Women's Corps, which is known in Hebrew as *chail nashim* but usually referred to in its abbreviated version, *chen*, which translates literally as charm and grace. This is not merely a linguistic coincidence. In fact, during their basic military training, women are coached to emphasize their femininity and neat appearance; they even receive cosmetic guidance as part of their official basic training. Through an emphasis on national security and total social mobilization, the Israeli military has been implementing explicitly sexist policies toward women. Women in the military are expected to raise the morale of male soldiers and make the army a home away from home. This gendered division of labor and power was institutionalized in February 1981, when the Israeli military attorney general ruled that coffee making and floor washing are within the legitimate duties of military secretaries, the majority of whom happen to be women.[25]

The Israeli military should be seen as another site within Israeli society—albeit an exceedingly important one—where Israeli-Jewish women are expected to perform traditional feminine roles and duties; the only difference is that they do so in military uniform. Moreover, the patriotic rhetoric that has been deployed to obscure the daily realities of women in the Israeli military makes women's protest against their assigned roles in the army almost impossible. Any sign of resistance is likely to be interpreted as a woman's refusal to contribute her share to the most sacred institution in Israel, the military. Military service is the key to first-class citizenship in Israel, and obeying orders is the key to being a good soldier; to demonstrate their loyalty and fulfill their duties both as citizens and as soldiers, Israeli women must comply with the gendered division of labor and power and with the sexist practices that characterize the Israeli army.

Aside from gender inequalities, the Israeli military has reinforced class, ethnic, and racial inequalities as well. Although it was supposed to be a melting pot designed to transform people of various Jewish origins and different cultural and socioeconomic backgrounds into the desired model of the new Israeli citizen, its policies and practices have not only mirrored but have also restored existing differences and structured inequalities within Israeli society. As Nira Yuval-Davis points out, the Israeli military "is far from being the perfect 'melting pot' which Ben-Gurion dreamt it would be. Class and cultural distinction are well reflected within the internal stratification of the army."[26] For example,

Jewish women who come from families with Middle East origins (known as Sephardic or Mizrachi) have had quite a different relationship to the military than have either their male counterparts or women who come from families with European and North American origins (known as Ashkenazi). The different treatment of these two groups has been particularly evident in the criteria used by the Israeli military to excuse people from military duty.

Despite the mandatory recruitment law, only sixty-five percent of Israeli-Jewish women serve in the military. Twenty-five percent opt out on religious grounds, and the remainder includes women the army labels qualitatively unsuitable; that is, women who do not meet the minimum requirements for military service: physical fitness, a sound knowledge of Hebrew, a minimum level of education, and a certain level of performance on psychotechnic tests.[27] Another category of women released from mandatory military service includes married and pregnant women or women with children. These women are released even if they are in the middle of their service. Apart from a small, extremely religious group of Ashkenazi women, the majority of women not recruited into the Israeli military come from families with Middle Eastern origins and low socioeconomic status. The army justifies these selective exemptions by pointing out that it has no need for soldiers under a certain educational level. Yet men with similar backgrounds are recruited into the military and often provided with educational opportunities and special training.

In sum, the Israeli army has played a chief role in upholding the centrality of national security in Israel and a gendered division of power and labor. In addition, the army has maintained and often reinforced a myriad of other structured inequalities within Israeli society.

Gender and National Liberation

Masculine and feminine gender identities and normalized gender roles may become temporarily or permanently unsettled during such periods of change and transformation as in the course of national liberation struggles. This fluidity has been evident in the West Bank and Gaza Strip, particularly since the outbreak of the *intifada*. One such indication is the fact that Palestinian women's participation in street demonstrations, confrontations with Israeli soldiers, and their leading roles in their neighborhoods' popular committees have become much more acceptable. This shift in acceptability of women's roles and political participation, however, has not been presented as a transformation in gender roles but rather as a national emergency; women's resistance was treated by men and women alike as "national work" (in Arabic: *amal al-watani*).[28]

The Palestinian Declaration of Independence issued on November 15, 1988, included a "special tribute to the brave Palestinian woman, guardian of sustenance and life, keeper of our people's perennial flame."[29] This tribute must be understood as an attempt to cope with rapidly changing gender relations; it sought to resolve possible tensions between older and newer conceptions of Palestinian femininity by acknowledging women's contribution to the struggle on the one hand and by highlighting images associated with earlier notions of femininity on the other.

The same tensions often surface in women's attempts to reconcile their new activities and aspirations within the contours of the national struggle. As Deniz Kanchiyot points out "women participating in nationalist movements were . . . prone to justify stepping out of their narrowly prescribed roles in the name of patriotism and self-sacrifice for the nation. Their activities, be they civic, charitable or political, could most easily be legitimized as natural extensions of their womanly nature and as a duty rather than as a right."[30] This interpretation in no way diminishes the fact that women who choose to take an active part in the struggle for national liberation develop new political skills and often new political awareness as they constantly negotiate their roles with their male counterparts.

The Palestinian women's movement in the West Bank and Gaza Strip emerged as part of and in direct relationship to the national struggle of the Palestinian people to rid themselves of the Israeli occupation. An underlying assumption during the early days of the movement was that Palestinian women would gain their liberation in part because of their ability to play an important role in the progressive ranks of the national movement. This assumption served as the primary pretext for the massive mobilization of Palestinian women during the early stages of the *intifada*. According to Palestinian scholar and activist Eileen Kuttab, "during that period the Palestinian woman chalked up achievements and sacrifices which firmly established her historic place in the struggle against imperialism and Zionism. She strove to prove

10. Palestinian women harangue Israeli soldiers, Ramallah, Occupied West Bank. December 1988. *Courtesy Neal Cassidy, Impact Visuals.*

herself and to assert her presence, and to express her belonging and being part of a national struggle.[31]

The decline in the intensity of the national struggle—during the third year of the *intifada*, especially during and in the aftermath of the Gulf War—triggered a sense of disillusionment and caution among many Palestinian women activists. Women began to raise questions about the fact that "the intifada has no social program which could aid the development and institutionalization of women's role in the struggle and politics" and that "the national forces' awareness and information regarding the necessity of women's participation in the struggle for (national) liberation was not reflected in a parallel policy of liberating women from the traditional values which block them from actively participating in the revolution."[32] Thus, although Palestinian women's commitment to the struggle for national liberation has not changed, many women have begun to publicly express their concerns that despite their contribution, national liberation will be achieved

without significant changes in the status of women and in gender relations within the Palestinian community.

The surfacing of an uneasy relationship between national liberation and women's liberation made the discourse of national liberation
alone insufficient to inspire the Palestinian women's movement. Thus,
while most Palestinian women activists continue to argue that nationalist projects and women's liberation projects are interdependent and
inseparable they have begun to challenge the separation between "gender and women's issues" and "national politics." In doing so, Palestinian women have indicated that their struggles for gender equality and
women's rights cannot be hidden anymore between the lines of nationalist discourses. Contrary to the premature judgment of some feminists
in Europe and North America, many Palestinian women activists are
quite aware of the double standards and tensions that underlie their
participation in the national struggle.

Despite their commitment to the national struggle against the occupation and for a Palestinian state, women activists have vowed not
.to forget "the bitter experience of Algerian women who, despite their
major contributions to their national liberation movement, were barred
from political and other forms of public life after Algeria won independence from France."[33] In the past few years, analogies between the
struggles of Palestinian women and those of women in other national
liberation movements, in particular the struggle of Algerian women
against the French colonial occupation of Algeria, have become an integral part of daily discussions and strategizing sessions of Palestinian
women on the grass-roots level.[34] "We will not let what happened to
our Algerian sisters happen to us." This assertion—made by a young
Palestinian woman activist in response to a question from an American feminist about what will happen to Palestinian women after national liberation is achieved—is indicative of the growing awareness
among Palestinian women that the struggle for national liberation and
for gender equality are inseparable.[35]

Local Discourses of Resistance

The *intifada* opened up space for both Palestinian and Israeli-
Jewish women to articulate connections between gender and the

11. A Palestinian woman at the forefront of a PFLP demonstration organized to commemorate the third anniversary of the *intifada*. Ramallah, Occupied West Bank, December 1990. *Courtesy Eric Miller, Impact Visuals.*

Israeli-Palestinian conflict. Prior to the *intifada*, women on either side of the conflict rarely challenged the primacy of national discourses whether oriented towards security or liberation. Israeli-Jewish women operated within the confines of Israel's obsession with national security and its implications for women's lives. Palestinian women seldom called into question the gendered division of power and labor that underlaid prevailing notions of national liberation. The *intifada* facilitated the emergence of local discourses and strategies of struggle for many women, reflecting a gradual departure from the constraints and hegemony of nationalist discourses.

These local discourses are not grounded in a particular ideology or framework. They represent a search for context-specific frameworks that address the interplay between gender issues, women's concerns and the politics of the Israeli-Palestinian conflict. These local discourses, which are grounded in the daily lives and struggles of Israeli-Jewish and Palestinian women, represent attempts by women activists to link their struggle against the Israeli occupation of the West Bank and Gaza Strip with the struggle for women's liberation and gender equality.

What triggered the emergence of these discourses? What has motivated Palestinian and Israeli-Jewish women to become politically active and search for ways to link their struggles for gender equality with the broader political struggle for the resolution of the Israeli-Palestinian conflict? It is obvious that the *intifada* served as a significant turning point for women's political activism on both sides of the Israeli-Palestinian divide. Yet, what remains to be explored are the influences and processes that have facilitated the transformations in women's political perspectives and mobilization. These transformations, reflected in the perspectives of individual women as well as in the agendas, priorities, and strategies of struggle of Palestinian and Israeli-Jewish women's groups, can be usefully examined in relation to personal and political turning points in women's lives.

The Personal is Political

The phrase "the personal is political" was a popular slogan in the women's movement in North America during the 1960s and 1970s, emerging in the context of consciousness-raising groups. Women were urged to see their personal problems and disadvantages as an outcome of public patriarchy and sexist oppression, and thus, as political issues. The message was that one must work from the inside out. The self was the starting point for a growing awareness of collective political concerns. That is, the well-being and transformation of individuals was treated as necessary for the accomplishment of the broader goal of social and political change.[36]

In the decade of the 80s, however, a growing number of feminists in Europe and in North America called the popular feminist slogan into question for privileging the personal over the political. According to bell hooks, although the popular slogan "did highlight feminist concern[s] with self, it did not insist on a connection between politicization and transformation of consciousness."[37] In other words, the personal became political, but the political did not become personal. As Jenny Bourne argues, "the organic relationship we tried to forge between the personal and the political has been degraded that now the only area of politics deemed to be legitimate is the personal."[38]

In areas outside the cozy North American context, however, it is often the political that is deemed more important than the personal. As is evident from the literature on women's lives and struggles around the world, women who become politically active in their communities reach new levels of personal and political consciousness and awareness of the interconnectedness between the two.[39] This awareness requires an understanding of the complex relationship between history, politics, and the daily experiences and struggles of women.

To come to terms with this relationship, in the particular context of the Israeli-Palestinian conflict, we must pay close attention to the historical turning points and to particular experiences that have shaped the political perspectives and actions of Palestinian and Israeli-Jewish women activists. In other words, focusing on the experiences of women in the West Bank and Gaza Strip and in Israel, in relation to the historical trajectory of the conflict, enables us to examine the complex processes through which political perspectives are constituted and transformed.

Given the centrality of the Israeli-Palestinian conflict in the lives of people in the region, it is not surprising that the stories of Palestinian and Israeli-Jewish women activists have been shaped in direct relation to the conflict. By recording the particular historical moments that served as turning points in the development and the consolidation of women's political perspectives, we do not only challenge the exclusion of women's voices and perspectives from conventional accounts of the Israeli-Palestinian conflict but also contribute to the counter-hegemonic project of rewriting the history of the Israeli-Palestinian conflict from a new and previously marginalized perspective. Finally, since women's experiences are diverse and multifaceted, a discussion of personal and political turning points in their lives may uncover new practices and modes of resistance.

When asked about significant turning points in their lives, many Palestinian and Israeli-Jewish women activists tend to connect the major events of their lives with crucial political developments in the region. The fact that women do not separate between the personal, political, and historical dimensions of their social transformation confirms that given the centrality of the Israeli-Palestinian conflict, these dimensions are intertwined and indeed inseparable.

Consider for example the story of Radwa Basiir, a former Palestinian political prisoner. Born in Jerusalem in 1952, she grew up in a village near Ramallah and spent eight years in an Israeli prison. Basiir's political socialization started rather early; she recalls for example that at the age of four she knew the names of the countries involved in the Suez crisis in 1956.[40] Basiir decided at a young age to put all her energy into studying, in order not to end up like most women in her village "where the only idea was that a woman should marry and have a family."[41] She insists that her political commitment to and involvement in the Palestinian national movement was intertwined from the start with her struggle for dignity, equal rights, and self-determination as a woman.

On the other side of the Israeli-Palestinian divide, the conflict played an important role as well, shaping and transforming women's personal lives and political perspectives. During the 1967 War, Israeli feminist and peace activist Dalia Sachs worked as an occupational therapist in the rehabilitation section of a major hospital in Israel. She insists that that particular experience was an important catalyst in the development of her political perspective.[42] The traumatic personal encounter with dead and injured Israeli soldiers made her critical of that particular war and later of all wars. The realization that "the people in power did not have any intentions to withdraw from the territories they occupied during the war," gradually prompted her to become more involved politically.[43] Although she joined what was then a tiny peace movement, Sachs points out that she began to take leadership roles and publicly express her political views only with the development of her feminist consciousness and with the emergence of the Israeli women's peace movement following the outbreak of the *intifada*.[44]

In addition to highlighting effects of Middle East politics, most particularly the Israeli-Palestinian conflict on women's lives, these stories put a human face on the history of the Israeli-Palestinian conflict; they highlight issues and make connections that are often written out of conventional historical narratives of the conflict. The particular impact the conflict had on different women, and their own interpretations of their experiences, sheds light on the gendered dimensions of the Israeli-Palestinian conflict as well as on the structural disparities in power and privilege between Israelis and Palestinians.

The next four chapters look at the Israeli-Palestinian conflict from the perspectives of Palestinian and Israeli-Jewish women activists. In addition to tracing the history of Palestinian and Israeli-Jewish women's movements in relation to the historical trajectory of the Israeli-Palestinian conflict, these chapters highlight the diversity and multiplicity of voices among both Palestinian and Israeli women. Of particular interest in this context are the strategies, forums, and practices that have been used by Palestinian and Israeli-Jewish women to address the relationship between gender and the Israeli-Palestinian conflict and the gradual transformation in images of women that have been projected by different women's groups.

4

Palestinian Women's Resistance

History, Context, and Strategies

→ The recent outpouring of writing on Palestinian women in the West Bank and Gaza Strip has depicted the *intifada* as the major catalyst behind the massive political mobilization of women.[1] The popular Palestinian uprising has indeed made women's involvement in the forefront of the national struggle visible, created more opportunities for women who were not previously part of movement, and triggered significant changes both in the volume and magnitude of women's resistance. There has been a tendency, however, to overlook pre-*intifada* organizing. This is not only incorrect but also runs the danger of erasing, or at least underestimating, a long history of pre-*intifada* women's activism—a history that has shaped and still affects more contemporary currents of Palestinian women's activism.[2]

Despite the fact that Palestinian women have been politically active at least since 1917, organizing for social and political reforms and later playing an important role in the Palestinian national movement, the stories of their struggles have remained for the most part untold and unexamined. This problem, however, is not unique to the Palestinian case but rather representative of the relative lack of attention to women's history in general as well as in the particular context of the Middle East.[3] As Middle East historian Nikki Keddie points out, women's history in the region has been overlooked at least in part due to methodological constraints: "because historians, unlike social scientists, cannot construct their own research projects based on people who

56

can be directly observed, interviewed, or given questionnaires."[4] Instead, they have to rely "chiefly on written sources, which are heavily male oriented, and a great mass of documents needs to be unearthed or restudied with women's questions in mind."[5]

Aside from difficulties in locating the relevant documents and recovering women's narratives, two more particular factors have contributed to the absence of detailed historical accounts of Palestinian women's resistance in the region. The first involves the persistence of stereotypical representations of Middle Eastern women, and the second, the politics of the Israeli-Palestinian conflict. Until the outbreak of the Palestinian *intifada*, Palestinian women, like women from other parts of the Middle East, were stereotypically portrayed as passive and subservient victims, largely dependent on men and confined to the home. These orientalist portrayals were decontextualized as well as ahistorical; little or no attention was paid to their ongoing, multifaceted struggles to achieve control over their lives and to their political involvement in campaigns for social, economic, and political change.[6] The politics of the Israeli-Palestinian conflict have further complicated the study of Palestinian women's history. Because Palestinian historical narratives are often perceived as ideologically charged, it is possible that to avoid controversy and possible career retributions, fewer scholars have undertaken such studies.

Although recently there have been more attempts, particularly by Palestinian women and a number of sympathetic scholars to unearth Palestinian women's history, against this background, any discussion of Palestinian women's history may be interpreted as an attempt to provide a comprehensive account of women's voices, perspectives, and actions.[7] The objectives of this chapter, nevertheless, are far less ambitious. It seeks to explore the origins and evolution of Palestinian women's resistance in relation to the changing sociopolitical context in the region, particularly the different phases of the Arab-Israeli conflict. It examines the ideological and practical basis for women's political mobilization and their strategies at different points in time and focuses, in particular, on the implicit and explicit connections made between gender issues and the broader political challenges confronting Palestinian society.

This focus points to a major dilemma that according to Rosemary Sayigh involves the question of "whether or not there is a problem of women [that is] independent of the collective national problem, and what is the correct relation between the two."[8] Stressing the inseparability of these two sets of problems and the unavoidable dilemma they have nurtured, Sayigh concludes that, "any attempt to escape this dilemma leads either to a feminism that ignores the effects of Ottoman/British/Israeli oppression on Palestinian social/family structures; or to sterile nationalism without social content."[9] In seeking to confront rather than to avoid this dilemma, this chapter pays special attention to the implications of certain historical turning points, from 1917 until the outbreak of the *intifada*, on the lives and struggles of Palestinian women and in particular to their attempts to address the connections between gender, women's resistance, and the Israeli-Palestinian conflict.

Women Take Action:
The British Mandate Period (1917–1948)

The first attempts by Palestinian women to organize as women occurred during the dismantling of the Ottoman Empire by the colonial powers, Britain and France, and in conjunction with the rise of Palestinian nationalism.[10] In particular, Palestinian women mobilized alongside men against the 1917 Balfour Declaration, which affirmed Britain's commitment to facilitate the establishment of a national homeland for the Jews in Palestine and contradicted earlier promises of Britain to support Arab self-determination. Threatened by British support for the Zionist movement and its designs on their land, Palestinian women marched alongside men in massive demonstrations in Jerusalem, Haifa, and Jaffa.

During that period, women's activism did not take place within the frameworks of exclusive women's groups; women who mobilized in support of the national struggle were mostly related to men who were politically involved.[11] It was not until the beginning of British rule in Palestine, in 1921, that the first exclusively-female organization—the Palestinian Women's Union—was founded. The Union was headquartered both in Jerusalem and Haifa and played an important role in organizing demonstrations demanding the abrogation of the Balfour Declaration, a halt to Jewish immigration, and an end to the torture of Palestinian political prisoners.[12] The Palestinian Women's Union provided both the nucleus and a framework for later women's initiatives in Palestine.

In 1929, during a year of particularly widespread nationalist protest in which organized Palestinian resistance against both Zionist immigration and British rule increased, at least two hundred delegates from all over the country attended the first Arab Women's Congress of Palestine.[13] The conference empowered women to establish women's unions throughout Palestine in both large and small urban centers and to intervene more directly in the shaping of foreign policy. Of particular interest in this context is the relatively well-documented story about a delegation of Palestinian women who, following the Arab Women's Congress of Palestine, had presented a petition to the British High Commissioner's wife, demanding the abrogation of the Balfour Declaration.[14] Although no one has systematically researched the history of the Union after 1932, Rosemary Sayigh claims that "interviews conducted with a few surviving leaders emphasize continued activity in the face of mounting violence and insecurity."[15]

Palestinian women played an important role in the national movement during the 1936–39 Great Revolt, when Palestinians rose up both against the British and the Zionists. Women supported the strikes and boycott against British and Zionist goods, sold their jewelry and donated the money to the Palestinian fighters, hid political fugitives, carried food and water to the guerrillas in the hills, and transported weapons.[16] The difficult circumstances during that time placed a double burden on Palestinian peasant women, who in addition to their hard work at home had to replace the men in the field during the harvest period.[17] Women's political organizing during that period was largely spontaneous, erupting for the most part outside the scope of formal organizations.

Apart from their involvement in and contribution to the national, anti-colonial struggle, Palestinian women were also active in the charitable societies which were founded in 1920s and 1930s by middle-class Palestinian women. These women, according to Noha Ismail, "were strongly influenced by the missionary philosophy."[18] Helping the poor soon became one of the primary stated objectives of the charitable societies and because there were many poor women, it was a framework that enabled women to help other women and facilitated encounters between women of various backgrounds. Soon after their establishment, the charitable societies had become the largest and perhaps most legitimate framework for social and political organizing among Palestinian women.

A number of different interpretations shape our understanding of Palestinian women's roles and activism during this period. Hiltermann, for example, argues that "the role of women during the Mandate period was limited to relief work in times of crisis, when male fighters needed women to provide them with food, clothing, and arms, and to take care of the wounded."[19] Rosemary Sayigh on the other hand questions the view that Palestinian women's initiatives were merely auxiliary and supportive, arguing that there is not enough information to support these generalizations. She further argues that the fact that little evidence exists about women's initiatives around the "woman question" is not enough to determine that women's organizations did not have a clear position on this question, or on other social issues.[20]

Despite the lack of extensive historical research on Palestinian women's organizing prior to 1948, it seems, however, that even if Palestinian women did address issues related to women's rights and social status, they made no explicit attempts at that point in time to draw connections between issues of particular concern to women and the national struggle. These connections became more evident and perhaps unavoidable following certain political developments in the region that had clear and direct implications for women's lives, beginning with the aftermath of the 1948 war.

Women's Strategies of Survival: Under Jordanian and Egyptian Rule (1948–1967)

The 1947–48 war, which ended with the establishment of the state of Israel and the Jordanian and Egyptian takeover of the remaining Palestinian lands, had grave implications for Palestinian women's lives, as it had for the Palestinian community at large. Almost overnight, many Palestinians had lost their homes and land and had become refugees. The loss of land translated into the loss of a primary source of livelihood and forced many to flee to refugee camps or huddle with members of their extended families who had survived the disaster in the surrounding Arab countries.[21] The dispersion, relocation, and economic hardship ruptured women's lives and organizations as "poverty or reduced income confined women to their homes and forced them out to work."[22] As a result, "the number [of women] available for 'national work' was drastically reduced."[23]

Given these difficult times, there would seem little reason to doubt the prevailing view that there was a serious void in Palestinian women's activism between 1948 and the establishment of the GUPW in 1964–65. Rosemary Sayigh points out, however, that in spite of hard circumstances, there was some continuity in women's organizing and an exploration of new forms of activism.[24] Several branches of the Palestinian Arab Women's Union, mostly those located in historic Palestine (Jerusalem, the West Bank, and Gaza), survived while few others were carried outside and reformed in the newly created Palestinian diaspora. But the various frameworks of women's organizing faced numerous political obstacles as restrictions were imposed on their activities by the Jordanian, Syrian, and Egyptian governments.[25]

Despite these obstacles, Palestinian women remained politically active. In addition to working within already existing religious and mostly charitable organizations, they established at least nine new social associations to deal primarily with the magnitude of the refugee disaster.[26] This upsurge of women's activism was affected at least in part by the political and economic dynamism that swept the Arab world during those years as a result of Nasser's defiance of Western hegemony and the rise of Arab nationalism. Consequently, educated and unmarried women, mostly from upper-middle-class backgrounds, joined opposition parties in the Arab world and in Israel.[27]

Open participation by Palestinian women in mixed-gender forums reflected a transformation in prevailing understandings of gender roles and gender relations within Palestinian society. This transformation had its origins both in the weakening of the extended family as the most powerful social institution in Palestinian society, which was a direct result of the 1948 disaster and dispersion, and in the spirit of social and political transformation that Arab nationalism nurtured. The new political reality, along with a high value placed on higher education (including that of women) and the harsh economic situation, which made the survival of many families dependent on women working outside the home, facilitated the development of women's political consciousness and inspired new modes of women's resistance. Although admitting that "only a small minority of women were politically

active during the 1948–67 period," Sayigh stresses that "their importance as a vanguard went far beyond their numbers."[28]

The establishment of the PLO and the Palestinian Women's Association (PWA) in 1964, and of the GUPW, in 1965, marked a new
phase in Palestinian women's political activism. The PWA was founded
in the West Bank and soon thereafter sent delegates to the May–June
1965 meeting of the Palestine National Council (PNC) in Jerusalem.
Following its first conference, the PWA began to branch out to other
parts of the region and laid the foundations for the establishment of
the GUPW a few months later, in August 1965.

The GUPW's stated goals were "to mobilize the efforts of Palestinian women and to organize a progressive political women's organization within the framework of the Palestinian Liberation Organization
in order to represent Palestinian women everywhere and to defend
women's material and moral interests, as well as to improve their social, cultural, vocational and living standards in general, and above all
to achieve equality in all areas of social and economic life."[29] The scope
of activities of both the PWA and the GUPW included emphases on
raising women's political consciousness, education, literacy campaigns,
and training courses for women in sewing, first aid and nursing.

A year later in 1966, the Jordanian authorities banned both the
PWA and the GUPW, along with other groups and institutions affiliated with the PLO.[30] The PWA, nevertheless, continued to operate "as
a clandestine organization under the cover of various charitable societies in the West Bank."[31] The GUPW, on the other hand, moved its
headquarters to Cairo for a period of two years and then moved to Lebanon. After that, according to Laila Jammal, "the GUPW went underground in Jordan and continued to work and hold meetings."[32] Despite
these political obstacles, the goals, projects and strategies of struggle
of the PWA and of the GUPW laid the foundations to many practical
and theoretical frameworks that were instrumental in shaping women's
resistance to the Israeli occupation of the West Bank and Gaza Strip.

The Israeli Military Occupation:
Implications for Women's Lives and Struggles (1967–1978)

The Israeli defeat of the Arab armies in 1967 and the subsequent
occupation of the West Bank and Gaza Strip transformed the

predicament of Palestinian society and precipitated the emergence of a Palestinian resistance movement, which offered new frameworks for women's political involvement. Women, like the rest of Palestinian society, were forced to redefine their goals and organizations and to adjust their strategies to the new reality of military occupation.[33]

The Israeli occupation created 300,000 new refugees and was implemented through a heavy-handed policy of social, political, and economic repression. This policy involved systematic attempts to confiscate Palestinian land and included a campaign designed to destroy the pre-1967 socioeconomic system, dismantle existing social and political institutions, and detain popular leaders.[34] The harsh policies of land expropriation and control over water resources forced more and more men and women to shift from agricultural work to other types of labor. Many Palestinian men had no choice but to become migrant workers in Israel and in the Arab states, particularly the Gulf countries.

Palestinian women first tried to obtain work on family farms, and when this was no longer an option they joined the ranks of unskilled laborers either in Israel or in the newly-established Israeli factories in the Occupied Territories.[35] The burdens on women were great and almost unbearable at times. As Islah Jad points out, "in addition to the stress-provoking nature of the work they tended to find, which was temporary and dependent on the fluctuations of the Israeli market," women were under enormous psychological stress because they continued to be solely responsible for housework, child-rearing, and for the well-being of their families.[36]

The Israeli occupation confronted Palestinian women with at least three interlocking systems of oppression—as Palestinians, as women, and as workers. They were forced to simultaneously struggle against this triple oppression and at the same time explore new ways of coping with the overwhelming pressures and responsibilities imposed by the occupation. During this period, especially between 1967 and 1971, women's participation in the Palestinian resistance movement took new forms. Women took part in a wide range of activities from demonstrations and sit-ins to sabotage and as a result some were killed, imprisoned, and deported.[37] While on the whole, the number of women participating was still not that large, the continuous insurrection in Gaza from 1968 to 1971 did involve the participation of many women.[38]

At the same time, some women confronted the occupation through channels of the local charitable organizations and through the GUPW, which were both linked to the Palestinian leadership.[39] The women's charitable organizations emerged in the West Bank during the last years of the Jordanian rule and expanded during the first decade of the Israeli occupation. They enabled members to carry out community-based initiatives while trying to escape the close monitoring of the Jordanian and later the Israeli military regimes. These organizations provided a valuable social and organizational framework for many women during that time.

Among the largest, most widely-recognized, and perhaps most successful of the charitable organizations in the West Bank is the Society of Ina'sh Al-Usra (Family Rehabilitation) in Al Bireh, whose primary goal since 1967 has been to help women cope with the multifaceted impediments of the Occupation. One of the guiding principles of the organization has been to train women especially in the production of traditional embroidery. In addition, the society has assisted women facing harsh conditions such as deportation, death of a relative, or imprisonment of men in their families.[40]

Notwithstanding their commitment to helping Palestinian women by organizing literacy and educational programs alongside vocational courses, these charitable organizations had some liabilities. Recent accounts, mostly by Palestinian scholars and activists, have described the work of the charitable societies as "a philanthropic expression of middle-class values" and as reinforcing prevailing structures of gender inequalities.[41] Rita Giacaman argues that "women were being trained in jobs that serve as backup for men's work: to be good housekeepers and mothers; and to have as many children as possible because this is their *wajib watani* (national duty)."[42] Along the same lines, Islah Jad concludes that "women's issues were looked down on as not worth considering" and that "by linking their work to the general struggle of women at a strictly 'national' level, the charitable organizations were mobilizing women only sporadically and in a limited fashion."[43] Nevertheless, both Giacaman and Jad acknowledge that the work of the charitable societies set the stage for new frameworks for women's organizing, which tried to address some of the ideological and practical limitations of earlier modes of women's resistance.[44]

The "New" Women's Movement:
The Emergence of the Women's Committees (1978–1987)

The women's committees were founded in the late 1970s and early 1980s and are considered the backbone of what is often referred to as the new Palestinian women's movement.[45] Their establishment, however, did not occur in a social or political vacuum but rather during a period that marked a great surge in national resistance and saw the emergence and activism of the student movement, trade unions, and numerous professional associations. Against this background, some women activists held a meeting on March 8, 1978, International Women's Day, which resulted in the establishment of the Women's Work Committee (WWC). The founders were part of a new generation of women—university-educated, politically aware and socially progressive. They grew up under Israeli occupation, were active in various voluntary work camps and increased their political involvement after the 1976 municipal elections in which women were allowed to vote for the first time.[46]

The women of WWC were determined to undertake initiatives that transcended the scope of membership and activities of the charitable societies and of other existing frameworks for women. They searched for new modes of organizing designed to "reach out to ordinary women, to help them understand their situation under occupation and overcome their disadvantages as women."[47] In order to meet their ambitious objectives successfully, WWC activists decided to first assess the needs of the women with whom they intended to work. To this end, they carried out two surveys in the Ramallah and al-Bireh area: one among working women employed in local workshops and the other among housewives.[48] The surveys were designed to determine whether the initial objectives set by WWC indeed reflected women's needs and wants and to develop strategies for recruiting these women into WWC as well as into the trade-union movement.

The WWC tried to reach out to the masses of women outside urban areas, primarily in villages and refugee camps. The plan had a clear rationale: in order to produce material and design projects that would be relevant to the daily experiences and struggles of women outside urban centers, WWC activists had to meet these women. The encounter shocked many WWC activists, who, as Philippa Strum notes,

"were astonished to discover a population totally outside their experience."[49] They found that a large proportion of the women in the villages and refugee camps were "illiterate, overworked, poor, economically
dependent on men, unaware of their legal rights, and focused entirely
on the private domain of home, cooking, cleaning, and children."[50]

Overall, this new mode of organizing yielded promising results:
the WWC "succeeded in attracting a following and in encouraging others to join the union movement."[51] At the same time, following their
eye-opening encounters with women in villages and in refugee camps
WWC activists realized that some of the women they met carried a
burden that was too great to permit their immediate mobilization for
political activities. Nevertheless, the surveys and the follow-up field
work reaffirmed the importance of the grassroots level, not only for
massive political mobilization of women but first and foremost for their
own professional development and political education as they were
finally able "to get acquainted and link up with real people, the rural
majority," which amounted to nearly seventy percent of the people.[52]

This new awareness among middle-class Palestinian women activists and the emphasis on grassroots projects and organizing had a
great influence on the development of WWC and later on the entire
Palestinian women's movement. Consequently the WWC adopted a
platform demanding "improvement in women's political, economic,
social and cultural status as part of the process of liberation from all
forms of exploitation."[53] For the first time, the Palestinian women's
movement was engaged in a somewhat open debate on the relationship between gender inequalities and other forms of exploitation and
between women's liberation and national liberation.

During the course of this debate in the early 1980s—which took
place amidst broader discussions within the Palestinian national movement over ideology and modalities of struggle—some of the differences
within the women's movement began to surface. Initially, the WWC
adopted a broad nationalist platform without, however, affiliating with
any of the four main factions of the PLO. But this did not last long.
Even though women's political affiliations did not play a central role
in the early mobilization and activities of WWC, a partisan power
struggle soon emerged within its ranks. This fragmentation was not
unique to the women's movement; trade unions confronted similar challenges during the same time.[54]

The WWC became explicitly associated with the political platform of the Democratic Front for the Liberation of Palestine (DFLP),
which led some members of WWC who disagreed with the pro-DFLP
line to establish new committees affiliated with other PLO factions.
Thus, pro-communist party women established the Union of Palestinian Working Women's Committees (UPWWC); women favoring the
platform of the Popular Front for the Liberation of Palestine (PFLP)
founded the Union of Palestinian Women's Committees (UPWC); and
pro-Fatah women established the Women's Committee for Social Work
(WCSW).[55]

Although some Palestinian women saw the split as a major im-
pediment to the unity of the women's movement, others argued that
the existence of more than one women's committee creates honest com-
petition, offering women more options and spurring overall recruitment
for the Palestinian women's movement.[56] Indeed, it appeared that despite the split along partisan lines, the women's committees tried to
avoid the type of rivalry, conflicts, and factional politics that characterized other sectors of the national movement, such as the trade
unions. This may be partially due to the fact that the four women's
committees—especially WWC, UPWWC and UPWC, which shared
a broadly socialist platform—had a similar analysis of the problems confronting Palestinian women and similar strategies for organizing and
mobilizing women. Given what they had in common, the women's
committees made conscious attempts to coordinate their work.

In 1984, the committees set up an informal network designed to
coordinate their responses to the pressures of the Israeli occupation and
its direct impact on Palestinian women's lives. Based on their success,
they then called for unity in the broader national movement.[57] It remains unclear, however, whether women engaged in these initiatives
were motivated primarily by the urgency to create a united national
front, or whether they saw factional politics as diverting energy and
attention away from the problems facing the Palestinian women's movement or whether it was a combination of both.

During the 1980s, all four women's committees carried out
projects, mostly at the grassroots level, designed to improve women's
socioeconomic situation and to increase their education. These projects
included vocational training, literacy courses, and health education
for women in villages and refugee camps as well as helping to spur

unionizing of women workers, setting up of new production cooperatives and establishing new nurseries, kindergartens, and mother-child
health centers throughout the West Bank and Gaza Strip.[58] All these
projects were implemented in a climate that was far from ideal. In addition to the standard problems of obtaining funds, mobilizing women,
and confronting prevailing attitudes against their participation in public
life, the women's committees had to deal almost on a daily basis with
harassment by the Israeli military.[59]

In sum, the new women's movement represented a dramatic departure from earlier modes of women's activism. Perhaps the most significant change involved the gradual shift from a movement that
appealed primarily to upper-middle-class women to a movement that
was becoming more class-conscious and grassroots-based. This change
in the social composition and class structure of the new women's movement was reflected both in its objectives and in its strategies. The movement sought to reach out to ordinary women, especailly to women in
villages and refugee camps.

The women's committees made their commitment to improving
women's lives explicit. The daily lives and experiences of women were
treated as a crucial dimension of the Palestinian struggle. Although resistance against the occupation remained a top priority, for the first
time, Palestinian women began to examine and confront the effects of
the political situation on their lives as women. This emphasis created
a context and planted the seeds for future discussions concerning the
relationship between the struggle for national liberation and that for
women's rights and gender equality that became widespread following
the outbreak of the *intifada*.

5

Palestinian Women and the Intifada

➔ As the previous chapter pointed out, a long history of women's political involvement and organizing produced the basis upon which responses to both the hardships and the opportunities of the *intifada* were predicated. The infrastructure of the women's committees was already in place and provided from the earliest stages of the uprising a framework and leadership for the swift and massive mobilization of women. The women's committees were not entirely surprised by the *intifada* and thus were quick to respond; when motivated women approached the committees and indicated their willingness to contribute, the framework was already there.[1]

In addition, Palestinian women's participation in the *intifada* bore the fruits of almost ten years of grassroots organizing and consciousness-raising. The *intifada* provided women who had participated in literacy programs or in skill-training courses operated by the women's committees with a golden opportunity to officially join the women's movement and to put what they had learned throughout the years to use. This generated a remarkable change in the composition of the Palestinian women's movement; those who participated in direct confrontations with Israeli soldiers, especially in villages and refugee camps, were no longer only students and longtime political figures, but rather women of all ages and from all sectors of society.[2]

Women's Resistance During the First Years of the *Intifada* (1987–90)

Women's participation remained consistently strong throughout the *intifada*, although the nature of their roles changed over time.

12. A Palestinian women's demonstration for International Women's Day, Jenin, Occupied West Bank, March 1990. *Courtesy Jonathan Lurie, Impact Visuals.*

During the first three months—a period of mass national mobilization characterized by embryonic and often spontaneous modes of organizing and leadership —women took to the streets to join numerous demonstrations and marches organized by the women's committees. Women of all ages and social classes threw stones, burned tires, transported and prepared stones, built roadblocks, raised Palestinian flags, and prevented Israeli soldiers from arresting people. Political participation by women, which at times involved confrontations with the army, was most intense in refugee camps, villages, and in the poorer neighborhoods of towns.[3]

The experience, social legitimacy, and institutional base of the women's committees enabled mass participation by women in the *intifada*. Day-care centers, that had been established by the committees throughout the West Bank and Gaza Strip during the 1980s, changed their regular schedules: instead of operating on a five-and-one-

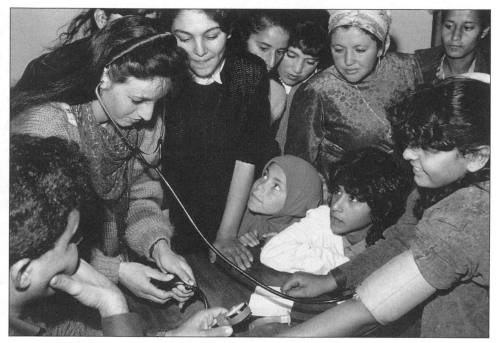

13. A Palestinian woman doctor teaching a first aid class for women in the village of El-Khadir, Occupied West Bank. *Courtesy Neal Cassidy, Impact Visuals.*

half-day schedule, they were kept open seven days a week and to late hours. Of particular significance during this stage was the health-education training that many women had received over the years; this training became indispensable as casualties mounted. According to a women's committee report, women "in villages, camps and cities have taken in the injured and administered first aid whenever possible in an attempt to prevent the inevitable arrests at hospitals."[4] But as the *intifada* moved into the next stage, the patterns and forms of women's participation changed, as did the responses of different groups within the Palestinian community.

The magnitude of women's resistance marked a significant trans-formation in gender roles; modes of behavior that were not deemed socially acceptable prior to the *intifada* became commonplace. Yet, the lasting effect of this transformation should not be overestimated.[5] In retrospect, it seems that the relative fluidity in gender relations and roles that occurred during the first months of the *intifada* was a by-product of the massive Palestinian response to the new reality introduced by the uprising.

This type of response to a political crisis is not unique to the Palestinian community. Literature on women's participation in broader political struggles points out that social crisis draws women into community and political activity, thus challenging the rigidity of prevailing notions of femininity, masculinity, and gender relations. At the same time, it appears that in most cases these challenges fail to yield long-term transformations in either gender roles or relations as communities tend to fall back on preestablished gender hierarchies once they overcome the initial reaction to the crisis.[6] This retreat to the prevailing notions of gender relations in the community prior to the crisis is not only a statement about gender. Rather, it reflects the community's attempts to readjust by embracing modes of social behavior that are familiar and thus associated with stability and survival.

During this crisis, however, Palestinian women's struggles for voice and visibility reached an important peak. Women seized the opportunity not only to demonstrate their contribution to the national struggle but also to assert themselves as women. What was the response of the Palestinian community to the new definitions of womanhood and gender relations that accompanied the massive participation of women in the early stages of the *intifada*? According to Islah Jad, women's massive participation in the uprising during its early months was acknowledged by most segments of Palestinian society, and women were urged by the Palestinian national leadership to continue to play an active role in the Palestinian resistance movement.[7] Judging from the initial response, women's participation was not perceived as a challenge to social stability but rather as a necessary and valuable contribution to the national struggle. At the same time, in the spirit of the spontaneous popular nature of the struggle at that stage, the women's committees did not articulate a clear agenda specifying the form women's participation should take.[8]

The *intifada* entered its second stage around March 1988. This stage lasted about a year and was characterized by the establishment of a local institutional infrastructure in the occupied West Bank and

Gaza Strip. Of particular significance was the founding of the Unified National Leadership of the Uprising (UNLU) and the establishment of the popular committees. The UNLU, representing all the factions of the PLO, was immediately declared illegal by the Israeli military. It remained underground and led the *intifada* via regular communiques; directives were implemented through the expanding network of popular committees. Five principle popular committees dealt with agriculture, education, food storage, medical, and guarding and each neighborhood or village created its own local committees to address these concerns.[9]

Popular committees soon became the most practical mechanism for political mobilization and for the preservation of the community. For many Palestinians the committees represented the infrastructure of the future Palestinian state or at least transient institutions designed to govern the community during the *intifada*. The committees resembled the women's committees in structure and in orientation. Indeed, there is clear evidence that the women's committees lent their experience and leadership to the establishment and expansion of the popular committees, to the extent that in some places "the work of the women's committees and the popular committees became indistinguishable."[10]

Rema Hammami, however, argues that this stage of the *intifada* was also characterized by a relative withdrawal of women from active political participation in the struggle and by a gradual move toward a gendered division of labor and power in the popular committees. Many women were forced to return to the primary roles they had before the *intifada*, which included mainly teaching and homemaking—more in line with prevailing notions of womanhood and gender relations. The prolonged closure of Palestinian schools and the massive imprisonment of Palestinian men were among the major factors that contributed to the retreat of active women's participation at the forefront of the *intifada*. The move toward a more gendered division of labor in the popular committees was reflected in the fact that women were active mostly in the education committees. There were hardly any women in the guarding committees, which formed the basis for what later came to be called the popular army, occupying an important and prestigious role at the decision-making level.[11]

There is no indication that women's participation in decision-making increased through their activism in the popular committees.

14. A Palestinian woman activist in an agricultural cooperative established by one of the Women's Work Committees. Sa'ir Village (near Bethlehem), Occupied West Bank, June 1990. *Courtesy Rick Reinhard, Impact Visuals*.

On the contrary, with time "women's role in the popular committees became an extension of what it traditionally had been in the society: teaching and rendering services."[12] Despite their progressive orientation and democratic decentralized structure, the popular committees "were used more as a means for maximizing the number of organized people than as instruments of social change."[13] Contrary to the expectations of many activists in the women's committees, women's participation in the popular committees did not result in a dramatic change in their social status or in a move toward gender equality in Palestinian society.

The realization that full participation in the national struggle does not necessarily guarantee an improvement in women's rights and social conditions triggered critical discussions within the Palestinian women's movement and in other progressive circles. This period of disillusionment sparked a strong sense of commitment to the struggle for gender equality and women's rights, and opened a new chapter in the history of the Palestinian women's movement. Palestinian women were determined to confront the obstacles that keep women and their concerns politically marginalized. Thus, they engaged in a process of assessing and rethinking their previous work as part of a search for new strategies of struggle and modes of organizing.

One of their first conclusions was that the women's committees needed to work more closely together. This resulted in the establishment of the Higher Women's Council at the beginning of 1989. The council was designed to serve as an umbrella organization for the major women's committees and to facilitate collaborative projects and enhance coordination. Another major conclusion was that the women's movement itself had treated the relationship between women's liberation and national liberation as self-evident, failing to articulate a clear position on gender issues and on problems that concern women within the broader struggle. As Palestinian scholar and activist Eileen Kuttab points out, women realized that "the Palestinian women's movement in general, and the women's committees in particular . . . did not formulate a clear social and democratic program which would speak to women's issues and work toward the solution of a portion of their problem."[14]

When it became clear that the Palestinian national movement was no different than most national liberation movements, in that it lacked the tools, frameworks, and motivation to seriously confront gender inequalities and discrimination within the movement and in the society, Palestinian women explored alternative ways to put gender and women's issues on the agenda of the national movement. One important result was that a number of new women's centers were established in the West Bank and the Gaza Strip.

New Women's Centers

The founding of new women's research, training and counseling centers represented another important step for the Palestinian women's movement. According to Lisa Taraki, these centers were the consequence of "the crystallization of what may be called a new feminist consciousness within the women's movement."[15] The newly established centers have offered both forums and new frameworks, enabling women to explore the complex relationship between national liberation and the emancipation of women. In addition to targeting specific problems which confront Palestinian women, these centers sought to develop both feminist consciousness and a feminist agenda which responds to the needs of Palestinian women.[16] For the first time, feminist theory and practice and references to women's struggles around the world became institutionalized as part of the ongoing debate within the Palestinian women's movement.

The forerunner of this new development was the Women's Affairs Center, established in Nablus in 1988 by Palestinian novelist Sahar Khalifeh. It sought to develop a feminist praxis that was context-specific and would resonate with the lives and struggles of Palestinian women in the Nablus area. Still in existence, the center's objectives are "to enhance the status of women in all walks of life by providing vocational and educational training, [and] conduct a wide range of research on women's issues."[17] The center offers computer training, English language and literacy courses, and publishes literature and magazines specifically addressing women's issues. More recently, the center initiated an action-research training course designed to prepare Palestinian women to carry out research for and about women.[18] Given the enthusiastic responses of women, the founders of the Nablus Center helped establish a similar center in Gaza in 1991 and are currently is in the process of training the staff of a third center that will soon be opened in Jenin.[19]

Another center that emerged during this period is the Women's Studies Center—also known as the Training and Research Society—which was founded in 1989 in the Jerusalem area. Similar in orientation and scope to the Women's Affairs Center in Nablus, it is committed to collaborative action research. The mission statement stresses its main objective: "developing both feminist consciousness and a feminist agenda which responds to the needs of Palestinian women."[20] The center is nonpartisan and works closely with all the women's committees as well as with women who have not been officially affiliated with any committee or political faction.

The Women's Studies Center offers training courses in research methodology and writing and holds workshops and lectures on such topics as "Women and Social Change," "Violence Against Women," and "Women's Health." In addition, the center has an active research agenda that includes projects on "School Dropouts" and "Women Laborers in Palestinian Factories." It also offers an impressive women-centered library and publishes *Al-Mar'a* (The Woman), the only Arabic-language monthly magazine in the West Bank and Gaza Strip and a bimonthly English-language magazine, *Sparks*, addressed primarily to women in the international community who have been supportive of the Palestinian women's movement.[21]

Inspired by the new wave of women's awareness and activism, women affiliated with the Bisan Center for Research and Development founded in 1990 the Women's Studies Committee. The committee sought to raise the level of women's involvement in decision-making and "to develop feminist thinking suitable for the Palestinian environment which will promote women's involvement in building Palestinian society at the social, economic, and cultural level."[22] A unique characteristic of the committees is its constant attempt "to bridge the gap between women active in the grassroots movement and female academics and professionals."[23] The Bisan committee has undertaken a number of projects including workshops and conferences, the publication of a comprehensive directory of Palestinian women's organizations, a survey on the needs of women's organizations in the West Bank and Gaza Strip, an evaluation of services for women offered by international non-governmental organizations in the Occupied Territories, and a research project on "The Impact of the Intifada on the Social Status of Women in Jalazoun Camp."[24]

All the projects carried out by these newly established centers are grounded in the conviction that Palestinian women experience oppression not only due to their national identity but also based on their gender and class identities, and therefore "for Palestinian women's emancipation, struggles must be waged on all these fronts."[25] The argument that Palestinian women suffer from a number of interlocking systems of oppression is not new. Yet the frameworks and strategies that have been explored by the newly established centers to confront this problem are fresh, innovative, and courageous. Most women's centers and projects work to raise women's awareness as women, as Palestinian citizens, and as workers in order to transform prevailing understandings of femininity, masculinity, and gender relations and to put women and gender issues on the agenda of the national movement and of the future Palestinian state.

Based on this shared rationale, the centers have explored different venues to achieve their objectives and have developed particular expertise on issues ranging from women's health and violence against women to women's involvement in the national decision-making process. With the establishment of the new centers, Palestinian women activists began to explore and redefine the meaning of "women's issues" in the West Bank and Gaza Strip in the context of an ongoing struggle against military occupation.

Women's Issues as Social and Political Issues

The term *women's issues* is generally used to refer to those issues that are thought to be of concern solely to women or have particular implications for women's lives. Although there has been a growing recognition that issues such as women's health, reproductive rights, and violence against women, for example, cannot be treated in isolation from other social and political questions, the responsibility and burden of addressing them have been assigned in most societies solely to women. Another problem, feminists have recently argued, is that narrow definitions of *women's issues* have been used to justify women's exclusion from domains that men have sought to maintain as their own primary positions of social and political power.

There has long been a consensus within the Palestinian women's movement that *all* issues are women's issues. Any issue that could be considered a women's issue has its origins in and has been shaped by the social and political fabric of Palestinian society under Israeli military occupation and thus is related to the broader political context. As a result, women have insisted that it is not simply women's responsibility alone to confront and resolve them. Despite the growing realization by Palestinian women that for too long issues central to their lives had been put on the backburner because they were considered simply women's issues, there was little public discussion around these issues prior to the establishment of the women's centers.

Determined to devote more attention to the particular problems and concerns that affected their lives as women, Palestinian women initiated numerous forums, research projects, and publications designed to explore the meanings of and strategies of dealing with women's issues in the Palestinian context. In this context, perhaps the most significant contribution of the Women's Studies Committee at Bisan was a conference organized in December 1990. Held under the title "The Intifada and Some Women's Social Issues," it was designed to provide women and men from a variety of political and ideological streams with a forum to discuss contemporary social and political issues and to explore possible solutions to these problems. The conference attracted about 450 women and fifty men and included scholars, researchers, and grassroots activists. This was the first time that some of the negative byproducts of the *intifada* for women's lives were discussed in a public forum.[26]

Initially, the conference's planning committee intended to focus on one particular issue—the pressure put on many women in the Occupied Territories to wear the *hijab* (headscarf).[27] But after much debate, the conference's organizers decided not to treat the imposition of the *hijab* as a problem in itself but rather as a symptom that ought to be explored in the context of a broader discussion of women's social issues during the *intifada*. This was a strategic decision, reflecting the rich experience, maturity, and level of sophistication of the Palestinian women's movement.[28] Another strategic decision was to invite prominent Palestinian men to make opening remarks at the conference.[29] The conference was designed to send an explicit message both to the national leadership and to the society at large: that the lives and struggle of Palestinian women deserved public attention.

The broad platform of the conference provided a forum for the discussion of other social issues that had affected women's lives during the *intifada*. Among the issues raised were the phenomenon of girls and women dropping out of schools and universities, which had resulted in a decline in the average marriage age, and the enormous burden carried by many Palestinian women who, in addition to participating in the national struggle worked to make the domestic economy self-sufficient and at the same time bore the brunt for raising children and maintaining the home.[30] Common themes throughout the conference were that women's issues are in fact social and political issues and that the struggle for women's rights and gender equality should be an integral part of the process of building a democratic Palestinian state.

The conceptualization of women's issues as social and political issues stressed the centrality of gender roles and gender relations in all spheres of life and opened up space for a critical exploration of different understandings of femininity, masculinity, and gender relations in Palestinian society. The conference and the public discussions it sparked on gender issues and democracy were part of a conscious attempt by women activists to hold Palestinian society in general and the national movement in particular responsible and accountable for improving women's lives. The anticipated response on the part of the Palestinian national leadership to this challenge was, however, once again superseded by unexpected political developments that relegated gender issues and the women's movement to secondary positions.

War, Peace, and Military Occupation: Implications for Women's Lives and Struggles (1991–1993)

The Iraqi invasion of Kuwait on August 2, 1990, and the subsequent deployment of American and international troops in the Gulf, took their toll on Palestinian society in the Occupied Territories and had direct implications for women's lives. The most immediate ones were economic. More than two hundred thousand Palestinians who had been employed in Kuwait fled, leaving behind all of their possessions. Only some were allowed back into the West Bank and Gaza Strip; most had to seek refuge elsewhere. As a result, most of the financial support sent by Palestinians in Kuwait to their families and to Palestinian institutions was cut off.

15. Young Palestinian women demonstrate against land confiscation. Occupied West Bank, June 1991. *Courtesy Paul Dix, Impact Visuals.*

The economic hardship was compounded by the serious political damage suffered by the PLO and the Palestinian community in the West Bank and Gaza Strip. Following Iraqi President Saddam Hussein's declaration that he would withdraw from Kuwait if Israel withdrew from the Occupied Territories—namely, the West Bank, the Gaza Strip, and the Golan Heights—PLO Chairman Yasir Arafat met with the Iraqi President a number of times as part of an attempt to serve as a mediator in the crisis. In this context, their casual embrace, which is customary among leaders in the Arab world, was misconstrued by the international media as unequivocal Palestinian support for the Iraqi invasion of Kuwait. As a result, Palestinians everywhere became victims of guilt by association. Up to that point, no official Palestinian, whether from the PLO or the Occupied Territories, had condoned the Iraqi occupation. On the contrary, Palestinian leaders in the West Bank and Gaza Strip published several statements condemning the occupation and calling for the Iraqi withdrawal. Nevertheless, there was virtually no interest on the part of the Western-based media to report such statements and present a more accurate picture of the Palestinian response to the Gulf crisis.[31]

Adding to the mounting pressure was sharp deterioration in living conditions following the October 8, 1990 massacre at the Haram al-Sharif compound in Jerusalem. Israel's notoriously brutal and quick-trigger border police shot and killed twenty one Palestinians, wounding more than one hundred, after Palestinians had gathered to defend the Islamic holy site from rumored extremist provocations by Israeli settlers from the West Bank.[32] Following Palestinian demonstrations of outrage against the massacre, the Israeli army contributed to the further escalation of violence by pouring more troops into the Occupied Territories. In addition, the occupation authorities sealed off the West Bank and Gaza Strip and forbade any Palestinian who had ever been placed under administrative detention from entering Israel. More than ten thousand Palestinians had received green identity cards that barred them from entering and working in Israel. At the same time, Israeli employers were encouraged to replace Palestinian workers with Soviet Jews.[33]

Despite difficult conditions, the Palestinian women's committees continued their regular work, and the Women's Studies Committee at Bisan was able to carry out the previously mentioned December 1990 conference on the *intifada* and women's social issues. As the United States' self-imposed January 15, 1991 deadline neared, however, women activists had to set long-term plans aside and gather all their energy to cope with the economic and political crisis and the prospects of a large-scale war in the region. Following the massive U.S.-led air attack on Iraq, the Israeli military administration imposed a devastating twenty-four-hour a day curfew on Palestinians in the Occupied Territories, which lasted a full month and a half.[34]

Soon after the curfew was imposed, the first Iraqi SCUD missiles were launched at Israel. On cue from Israeli media outlets, CNN was quick to report on those Palestinians who had cheered the Iraqi missiles from their rooftops. Little or no attention was paid to the fact that more than 1.5 million people were being held hostage in their houses, many on the verge of starvation, with no sirens and no gas masks to protect themselves against the possibility of an airborne chemical attack.[35] While images of Israelis in gas masks and Jews in sealed rooms

were omnipresent in international media coverage, with all their historical connotations, Palestinians in the Occupied Territories struggled
to survive with no money, food, or medicine and no one to bear witness. A particular difficult aspect of the prolonged curfew was that
people were cut off from one another and from their extended family,
community, and support networks. This imposed reality had negative
implications for women's organizing, based as it was on group decision-
making and networking. Women's committees and the women's centers, like all other businesses and institutions, remained closed, making
most Palestinian women who worked outside the home unable to continue their social and political work; instead they were forced to become full-time wives and mothers.

Just weeks before the actual ground war against Iraq was launched,
the Palestinian women's movement was shaken by an internal conflict
in the Palestinian Federation of Women's Action Committees
(PFWAC), one of the four major women's committees. Grassroots insurgents took over the PFWAC's building in Beit Hanina accusing the
head officer of not running the committee democratically. The result
was a split, with the two groups claiming title to the committee's name
and ongoing projects. According to the insurgents, the conflict reflected
the chasm between the elite women who headed the committee and
the women who worked at the grassroots level. At the same time, it
was clear that the split was affected in part by a broader ideological
split within the DFLP, the PLO faction with which that PFWAC was
affiliated, over the preferred solution to the Israeli-Palestinian conflict.[36]
As a result, intense internal discussions began in other committees on
the relationship between the grassroots and the elite as well as on the
relationship between the women's committees and the various political factions of the PLO.

In the aftermath of the war, the Jerusalem-based Women's Studies Center started a research project on the effect of the Gulf War on
Palestinian women in the West Bank and Gaza Strip.[37] A few months
later in July 1991, the center organized a conference on domestic violence against Palestinian women, the first of its kind in the Occupied
Territories. The conference featured two papers followed by a lively discussion. First, Nadera Kivorkian discussed her field research on how
women in the Jerusalem District perceive the problem of husbands' violence against women. The second paper, "Theoretical Considerations

Regarding Violence Against Women," was presented by Dr. Hala Attalah from Birzeit University.[38]

The subsequent discussion focused on the ways in which women could address domestic violence and resulted in a list of recommendations and in the establishment of a ten-member follow up committee.[39] The conference dealt with the sociocultural context of domestic violence but little attention was devoted to the connections between violence against women and the broader political context of the Israeli occupation. Consequently questions concerning the possible effects of the six-week curfew in the Occupied Territories during the Gulf on domestic violence or concerning the relationship between the violence inflicted daily on Palestinians by the military occupation and domestic violence, were underplayed.

An exception was Kivorkian's study which addressed the impact of the *intifada* on violence against women in the Palestinian community. It pointed to a *lower* frequency of domestic violence in Palestinian homes, that had experienced direct violence at the hands of the Israeli military during the uprising—families where someone had been killed, wounded, or imprisoned by the Israeli military.[40] No attempt was made, however, to interpret this relationship or to explore the relationship between economic constraints, especially in the aftermath of the Gulf War and the phenomenon of violence against women. Nevertheless, the conference not only placed domestic violence against women on the agenda of the women's movement and provided a public forum for its discussion, it also redefined violence against women as a social problem.

Indeed, the conference triggered not only an ongoing discussion on the topic of violence against women, but also the founding of social institutions such as a new counseling and consultation project for women in Nablus as well as training courses, sponsored by the women's committees and centers. As part of the analysis of the problem, women activists drew from feminist literature and models of activism concerning violence against women around the world. The UPWWC, for example, sent a representative to take part in a training course organized by the U.S.-based Center for Global Issues and Women's Leadership, which dealt with violence against women in different contexts and societies and focused on how to share experiences and develop strategies to deal with it. The UPWWC also printed in its newsletter a copy of an international petition demanding that violence against women be recognized as a violation of human rights. Signed by Palestinian women in the West Bank and Gaza Strip, the petition was presented to the 1993 United Nations World Conference on Human Rights.[41]

Another topic that was high on the Palestinian women's agenda in the aftermath of the Gulf War was how to respond to the peace process set in motion by the United States. Just as the Palestinian community was divided, the women's movement was neither unified nor clear about its stand on this process. The issue was not whether peace was wanted or not, but rather what kind of peace could be obtained under this format and what implications it would have for women's lives. Following the November 1991 Madrid conference, which brought together Israeli and Arab representatives for the first time, the women's committees hosted Hanan Ashrawi and Zahira Kamal, both members of the Palestinian delegation to the talks. In addition to providing women with information about the peace process, the discussion focused on the need to strengthen the role of Palestinian women in the political arena and in the decision-making concerning the peace process.[42]

Despite cautious optimism expressed by many women following the Madrid conference, the focus of the Palestinian national struggle shifted almost entirely from the grassroots level to the level of international diplomacy. As a result, women's contributions and participation were marginalized once again. The political skills and experience that Palestinian women had acquired in the course of their ongoing struggles, their special concerns, and their perspectives and visions for peace in the region were overlooked both in the composition of the Palestinian delegation and on its agenda.

The exclusive focus on international diplomacy as the only viable mean to resolve the Israeli-Palestinian conflict triggered feelings of confusion and frustration among Palestinian women activists, who felt that their activism at the grassroots level was stripped of its political potential and significance. According to Eileen Kuttab, many activists found it difficult to "get back into action" and especially to encourage other women to do the same.[43] The frustration and confusion were related, at least partially, to the fact that the peace process interrupted almost two years of intense discussions and planning by the women's committees, women's centers, and representatives of various organizations, which had come together under the banner of a newly established Task Force on Women to formulate a united agenda. Given the new political context, some activists felt the only way to keep a women's agenda alive was to interject it into the official peace process.

As the Palestinian leadership established "technical committees" designed to outline the basic frameworks and policies for the future Palestinian authority, women activists pressured the leadership to put women's issues on the agenda of those committees. Finally, after more than six months, a Women's Technical Committee was founded. The women's committee, however, unlike the others did not receive its funds from the regular budget, but rather depended primarily on the financial support of a foreign donor.[44] Nevertheless, the new committee embarked on a rather ambitious journey, establishing several subcommittees to examine issues such as legislation, education, and employment, with the aim of making policy recommendations. In addition, the committee began work on a Women's Bill of Rights, which according to Giacaman and Johnson was "seen as a mobilizing tool to show the interests and strength of women prior to the introduction of key pieces of legislation, like a constitution."[45]

The Women's Technical Committee members saw themselves as part of a pressure group rather than as official members of a quasi-governmental body. They consulted frequently with the women's committees, women's centers, and grassroots activists. But following the massive deportation of 415 Palestinians in January 1993, and the March 1993 blockade-style Israeli closure of the Occupied Territories, the relationship of the Women's Technical Committee with the women's movement, and especially with women on the grassroots level was strengthened.[46] Many Palestinians, women in particular, grew suspicious after twenty months of a so-called peace process that had only resulted in harsher oppressive measures and more suffering and misery.

The spring and summer of 1993 marked a period of intense political debates within the Palestinian community on the future of the peace talks, accompanied by increasingly harsh criticism of the undemocratic practices of the PLO leadership in Tunis.[47] As the details about the Gaza and Jericho First plan were made public and following the signing of the Declaration of Principles, the public debate concerning the future of the peace talks escalated into a serious conflict between Palestinians who supported the agreement and those who opposed it.[48]

The women's movement also was and remains divided between individuals and groups who back the agreement and those who oppose it—primarily those committees and projects affiliated with the PFLP and with Nayef Hawatmeh's faction of the DFLP. After women opposed to the agreement argued that they could not work anymore under the banner of the technical committee, they ceased to be invited to other initiatives, such as demonstrations, launched by the other women's committees, against the closure and the deportations. During this period, the women of the opposition directed their energies toward the creation of a united opposition bloc. According to grassroots activist and organizer Maha Nassar, the founding of an opposition bloc was not a result of "unification from above," initiated by the leadership of PFLP and DFLP, but rather "a process which arose from below, from popular organizations and institutions such as the trade unions and the women's committees."[49]

Yet within the broader response to the peace process and the Oslo Accord the women of the opposition found themselves part of an uneasy alliance with Hamas, the major Islamist group in the West Bank and Gaza Strip. The two groups share a similar critique of the Gaza Jericho plan which is seen simply as a device to legitimate the permanent Israeli control of Palestinian lands and to disempower those who have long struggled for Palestinian self-determination. It was clear from the outset, however, that the opposition bloc and the Islamist forces have different visions about the character of any future Palestinian state. These visions of course involve also different understandings of femininity, masculinity, and gender relations. Women activists from the opposition bloc are quite aware of the possible implications of this alliance, which they refer to as both dangerous and temporary. Nevertheless, given the current political situation they treat this unexpected alliance as inevitable.[50]

New political circumstances forced women in the opposition to keep their positions on women's liberation and social issues separate from their political stands on the Israeli-Palestinian conflict. Though apprehensive, they are determined not to let the strategic political alliance with Hamas affect their social platform or their commitment to gender equality.[51] The alliance between the women's committees who support the peace agreement and the Palestinian leadership is in many ways equally problematic, dangerous and full of contradictions. Women

who have sided with PLO factions supporting the Declaration of Principles are far from being satisfied with the representation of women and
their concerns in the Palestinian delegation and in the technical committees. In both cases women have reacted to a current political development based on their party loyalties and their positions on the
Israeli-Palestinian conflict. At the same time, women activists on both
sides of the political divide are aware that they must stay vigilant and
protect their agenda on gender and social issues.

In conclusion, although many Palestinian women were already
aware prior to the *intifada* that theirs was a two-fold struggle, for
national liberation on the one hand and for women's rights and gender equality on the other, the uprising created a context for raising new
and difficult questions about the relationship between the two. During the first two years of the *intifada* the emphasis on women's rights
and equality remained consistent for the most part; women activists
were convinced that the volume of their participation in and contribution to the national struggle would inevitably result in a significant
transformation of their position in society.

This conviction weakened, however, as women increasingly
realized that their full participation in the struggle for national liberation did not necessarily guarantee improvements in their social and
political status. The common tendency to prioritize the national
movement's agenda over their own was replaced by a growing awareness that what were called "women's issues" should be an important
component of the national struggle and by an urgency to develop and
make explicit a women's program. The founding of research, training
and counseling centers throughout the West Bank and Gaza Strip
between 1988 and 1991 represented an important step in that direction. But as a result of the social and political impact of the Gulf crisis
and subsequent war, the excitement that accompanied the new initiatives of the women's movement could not be sustained. This turn of
events serves as a clear reminder that political developments at the
international level often have direct implications for women's lives and
struggles.

In the aftermath of the Gulf War, women activists resumed their
efforts to reconceptualize "women issues" as social and political issues
and to outline and implement projects that will improve the lives of
Palestinian women, especially those living in small villages and refugee

camps. This time, however, women's efforts were disrupted by peace rather than by war. The U.S. sponsored Madrid Conference and the later Oslo Accord and Declaration of Principles signed between the PLO and the Israeli government became the major topics of political discussions and concerns within the Palestinian community, both in the Occupied Territories and in the diaspora. In addition to dividing the Palestinian society into supporters and opponents of these developments, the exclusive focus on the narrow parameters of international diplomacy marginalized grassroots work for social and political change in general and women's efforts in particular.

Once again, the Palestinian women's movement has been forced to assess and rethink its previous work and search for new strategies of struggle and modes of organizing. Some women are convinced, however, that in order to successfully cope with the present crisis and prevent future ones caused by political developments both at the local and at the international level, the movement ought to pay closer attention to the relationship between gender and the political context of the Israeli-Palestinian conflict. This implies that when confronted with a crisis situation, instead of reacting simply on the basis of prior political affiliations, the women's movement will facilitate public discussions to assess the impact of a particular development on women's daily lives and to explore potential ways of coping with the crisis. Based on such analyses of the Israeli-Palestinian conflict and the implications of different plans for its resolution for their lives and struggles, women might put forth alternative visions for social transformation and peace-building in the region.

6

Israeli-Jewish Women's Struggles

History, Context, and Strategies

➤ Two popular images have shaped the way women in Israel are viewed. One is the tough, powerful, and exceedingly unfeminine Golda Meir, the former Israeli prime minister; the other is the sexy, exotic woman soldier, in military fatigues with a machine gun slung over her shoulder, ready to fight for her country. These images have fueled a myth about gender equality and women's political participation in Israel, which, unfortunately, has helped reinforce the marginalization of women within Israeli society and politics. The equality myth, however, has not gone unchallenged. The great discrepancy between these images and the actual lives of Israeli women has resulted in numerous attempts by women in Israel "to call the equality bluff" by detailing the institutionalized gender discrimination they confront every day in Israeli society.[1]

More important than simply proving the myth to be false is understanding how it has been formed, which has been in direct relation to the historical trajectory of the Arab-Israeli conflict. The image of the liberated and sexy woman soldier, for example, became particularly popular after the 1967 war, nurtured both in Israel and abroad to garnish Israel's victory. One the one hand, the public display of Israeli women soldiers was intended to emphasize that Israel was fighting for its very existence and therefore women had to contribute to the national effort. On the other hand, women's participation in the military was also presented as proof of the modern and democratic character of Israel. This image of the allegedly liberated, modern Israeli woman soldier was then contrasted with images of veiled, powerless Arab women in order to depict the neighboring Arab countries as undemocratic and culturally backward, thus demonstrating Israel's role as an outpost of the West.

The second image associated with Israeli women—that of former prime minister Golda Meir—is also related to the politics of the Arab-Israeli conflict in that it was used mainly abroad to mobilize support for Israel. The powerful woman prime minister came to stand as a symbol for a supposedly progressive society fighting for its survival. Despite her coarse personality and tough rhetoric, the very fact that she was a woman rather than a retired general made Israel appear more vulnerable and thus generated more sympathy abroad. In particular, it helped obscure Israel's militaristic ethos, with its aggressive posturing and tendency toward territorial expansion. Even more damning to the progressive connotations of Meir's leadership for women was that she was no champion of women's rights and was especially unsympathetic to the feminist movement in Israel whose initial crystallization began during her tenure.

Rather than accurately reflecting women's actual roles and positions in Israeli society, popular images such as those of Golda Meir and of Israeli women soldiers reflect the role of the Arab-Israeli conflict in generating idealized notions of womanhood. The formation and transformation of these images must be examined in direct relation to the political context and more particularly in relation to the history of the Arab-Israeli conflict. Equally important is to record the discrepancies between common representations of Israeli women and their actual lives.

In Search of a New Identity:
Jewish Women in Palestine (1911–1948)

The founding of the Women's Workers' Movement in 1911 represents the first example of Jewish women's political organizing in Palestine. Established within the Labor Zionist movement, it grew out of the disappointment of a small group of women with the limited roles assigned to them in the emerging society. These women had come to

Palestine to participate more fully in social life than they had been per-
mitted to do in the middle-class circles of their Jewish communities in Eastern Europe. They did not expect, nor had they prepared themselves, to
struggle for equal rights. As Dafna Izraeli stresses, "they thought equality
would be an accompanying feature of their move to the new homeland."[2]
Many of these expectations had their origins in the nationalist-socialist
ideology prevalent in the Zionist movement at the time.

Based on her examination of articles, diaries, and collected writings by women in Palestine during 1904–1914 and 1919–1923, Deborah
Bernstein concludes:

> "The most salient element in women's articulation concern-
> ing themselves was their identity as members of the new commu-
> nity, the new workers' society. Women repeatedly emphasized their
> belonging to and partnership in the community . . . Women saw
> only one way to achieve their aspiration, that is by taking part in
> all that was considered important in the new society. There were
> no different roles, criteria, and spheres for men and women. Thus
> women could achieve their fulfillment as women precisely by tran-
> scending gender differences, by embarking on action defined by
> its social, national and human significance."[3]

Reality, however, did not meet the expectations; women were
relegated to secondary roles in the new society. Farmers in the agricultural villages refused to employ women, considering them ineffi-
cient for workers and immoral for living on their own among men.[4]
This situation prevailed even with the establishment of the *kvutza*, a
small collective settlement in which all were to share equally in the
work.[5] Conscious and egalitarian efforts to transcend unequal divisions of labor within the Jewish community in Palestine did not
extend to women's work. Domestic work was still considered by many,
both men and women, as women's responsibility; women were auto-
matically assigned to the kitchen and the laundry. Gradually, women
came to realize that their desire to work in agriculture and be equal
partners in building the new society could not be realized through
the existing structures of the Labor Zionist movement.

Based on their disillusionment, seventeen women attended the
first meeting of women workers in 1911, in Kinneret, one of the first
cooperative agricultural settlements. The meeting presented women

workers with their first opportunity to share experiences and individual grievances and to extend moral support to one another. It also laid the foundation for the emergence of a Jewish women's movement in Palestine.[6] Yet it should be recognized, as Izraeli and others point out, that "from its inception, the Zionist women's workers movement avoided defining itself as engaged in a struggle against male oppression."[7] Instead, a need for "self-transformation" was stressed, emphasizing that to fulfill the ultimate goal of building a new society, "women must be helped to change so that they could contribute more effectively toward the realization of shared values and goals."[8]

During this period, Jewish women in Palestine struggled primarily for greater equality between men and women in the allocation of such scarce resources as immigration certificates and job opportunities and demanded greater participation in the decision-making bodies of the Labor Zionist movement and its affiliated organizations. In addition, they addressed particular problems confronting them as workers and provided agricultural training for women. The discourse of self-transformation and an emphasis on the value of working together as women became the primary strategies for achieving equal rights. Shared experiences and the unique problems and objectives of women became the primary basis for political organizing. The underlying assumption was that women could best achieve their goals by transcending gender differences and stressing their similarities with men.

The struggle for gender equality during this period involved a conflict between two competing projects: one designed to put women's self-transformation on the agenda of the Labor Zionist movement, and the other to turn the Women's Workers' Movement into a social service organization. The conflict came to a partial resolution in 1930 when the movement became more social service oriented and changed its name to The Organization of Working Mothers in an attempt to resolve the tensions between women's work outside the home and their roles as wives and mothers.[9]

This transformation gave legitimacy to a gendered division of labor and power. As a result, occupational training took on the task of preparing girls and women for socially-accepted feminine roles such as hairdressers, dressmakers, nursemaids and nursery teachers and left political decisions, trade union activities and economic policy in the hands of the male establishment. A number of interrelated factors led to this dramatic transformation in both the vision and the strategies of the Jewish women's movement in Palestine: (1) the exaltation of aggressive masculinity by both men and women; (2) the organization of production according to traditional definitions of gender roles; and (3) the centrality of mothering to women's identity and its conceptualization as a women's responsibility.[10]

The difficult conditions in Palestine at the time served to increase the importance of qualities considered masculine; physical strength became one of the first criteria for the distribution of social prestige and power within the community. Because physical strength was seen as a key to productivity, and given that the *kvutza* was fighting for recognition of its economic viability, women were defined from the beginning as being less productive than men. In their struggle for gender equality, women emulated the masculine model and sought "to make the functions, qualities and goals of men their own, without demanding a similar change on the part of men, without demanding that they 'feminize'."[11]

Organization of production according to principles of productivity and profitability helped solidify the development of two spheres of economic activity along distinct gender lines. Consequently, it became impossible for women to win the prestige enjoyed by men as full-time farmers—the true pioneer ideal, a central fixation of Jewish collective identity in Palestine. Within this broader context, which valued masculinity and profitability and directly linked the two, motherhood could only undermine the status of women. Fogiel-Bijaoui describes how "when the first children were born the care of the newborn was immediately entrusted to the mother. And even though demands were made here and there that fathers participate in the care of children, such a solution was never seriously considered. . . . It seemed totally dysfunctional and illogical within the realm of agriculture to exchange a man, a 'productive worker', for a woman, a 'less productive worker'."[12]

Another dimension crucial to understanding the struggles of Jewish women in Palestine during this period concerns the broader political context and its implications for women's lives. With the escalation of tensions between Zionists and Palestinians opposed to Zionist settlement in Palestine in the mid-1930s, the problem of gender equality was further marginalized and relegated to a secondary status. Many women acceded to this. Some contended, however, that equality of rights depended on equality of duties and therefore sought to participate in various paramilitary organizations which operated underground. Still, women's participation in these organizations was limited to auxiliary roles on the homefront; women were not allowed to take part in civil defense or in military operations.

During the 1936–1939 Palestinian uprising against British rule and Zionist settlement, women were once again denied the possibility to stand guard around the kibbutzim. This restriction sparked a women's rebellion in demanding their right to stand guard. It was swift and strong and quickly achieved its goal: in most kibbutzim women were allowed to stand guard. This rebellion is among the few successful examples of collective action by women designed to explicitly protest gender inequality in the pre-1948 era. Yet neither the success of this particular protest, nor the active participation of women in the Zionist project changed the gendered divisions of labor and power within the Jewish settlement in Palestine.[13]

The Militarization of Women's Lives (1948–1967)

Israel's 1948 Declaration of Independence made an allusion to gender equality, stating that "the State of Israel will maintain complete social and political equality for all it citizens regardless of religion, race or sex."[14] Nevertheless, the establishment of the state narrowed the little space women had to express their political views on general issues and to struggle against their discrimination as women. The "founding fathers" of the Jewish state, under the paternal leadership of Ben Gurion, established themselves at the center of Israeli-Jewish collectivity. In the aftermath of the war, and especially following the 1956 Sinai campaign, the military came to occupy a central institutional role in defining and reproducing the social and political fabric of Israeli society. As Natalie Rein points out "the army's needs were the country's needs and no other philosophy had the slightest chance of survival. Advancement on every field was dependent on performance in the army. It set the tone of life."[15]

The militarization of Israeli society was ushered in by the dynamic and charismatic personality of Moshe Dayan who, in 1953, became the army's commander in chief and whose authority on military matters remained virtually unchallenged for the next twenty years.[16] Dayan

became a symbol of the *Sabra*: militant, arrogant, and exceedingly masculine. His personal ethos coupled with his military "adventures" inspired an entire genre of heroic anecdotes that occupied a central role
in Israel's popular culture at the time. Dayan emerged as a primary role
model for Jewish men, representing a shift from a past of perceived helplessness and powerlessness associated with the European-Jewish experience to a present and future of personal and military prowess and
strength. Jewish manhood had been redeemed and redefined in terms
of an aggressively militarized national state.

The exaltation of masculinity was reinforced with the escalation
of the Arab-Israeli conflict and became linked not to profitability like
it was during the pre-state period, but rather to national survival and
national identity. The belief that Israel was a nation under siege provided the basis for maintaining national unity in the face of external
enemies, and men were assigned the primary role of safeguarding the
existence of the state. This shift in the individual and collective identity of Israeli-Jewish men had direct consequences for women's lives
and struggles at the time. Natalie Rein summarizes this period as one
where "the hopes and aspirations of Israeli women toward equality and
egalitarianism faded. The country turned its back on humanism and
pursued a policy of nationalism, militarism and Zionism."[17] From 1948
onward, women had no space to assert themselves outside the confines
of their role as male-supporters or to protest the erosion in their status. In order to be part of the Jewish state they had to constantly support and express gratitude for their male 'liberators' and 'protectors,'
thus accepting the gendered division of labor and power.

This was the climate in which David Ben Gurion helped institu-
tionalize an ideal of motherhood as the major venue through which
Israeli-Jewish women could contribute to the national project. "If the
Jewish birthrate is not increased, " Ben Gurion recounted in his pro-
jections at the time, "it is doubtful that the Jewish state will survive."[18]
In other words, while Israeli men defended Israel on the battlefield,
women were asked to secure Israel's survival on the homefront. Indeed,
Ben Gurion took this analogy further by comparing "any Jewish woman
who, as far as it depends on her, does not bring into the world at least
four healthy children" to "a soldier who evades military service."[19] The
analogy between women's "special" role as reproductive units and the
military service of men has defined the Israeli national project, with
its gendered assumptions and practices to this day.

With the militarization of motherhood and the additional national glory attached to the production of sons—that is, future soldiers—and given their limited access to decision-making levels of social and political institutions, women had few options other than the socially-accepted roles of wives and mothers. They did not mobilize to protest their collective social and political predicament nor did they take explicit political positions *as women*, especially not on questions of war, peace, and security. This non-mobilization can be attributed both to the absence of an organizational framework and to the broad political and social consensus taken by many as a sign of unity, essential to the survival of the nation.

Wars, Gender, and the Politics of Consensus (1967–1973)

The June 1967 war renewed and solidified the national and political consensus in Israel, reaffirming the centrality of the military and significantly strengthening Israel's relationship with the Jewish world in the diaspora. The war, which resulted in Israel's occupation of the West Bank, the Gaza Strip, and the Golan Heights, also marked a new stage in the construction of Israel's collective identity. According to former Israeli president Chaim Hertzog, it marked Israel's "transformation from a potentially helpless victim into a brilliant victor [and] created a euphoria which brought about a revolutionary change in Israel. Against the background of somber prospects a few days before, their incredible victory evoked a reaction throughout the Jewish world such as Israel had never known or experienced."[20]

The first war fought by the new generation of Israeli *Sabras* was interpreted as a major step towards leaving the past behind. Dominant accounts of the war in Israel's popular culture often contrasted images of the newly triumphant heroes with the helpless Jewish victims of the past. In many ways, crossing the pre-1967 border, known as the Green Line, and defeating "the enemies" across that border, marked the defeat of the enemy within—the passive and victimized Jew. The omnipotence of the Israeli military resulted in further militarization of Israeli society and the institutionalization of national security as the top social and political priority, which defined the meanings and boundaries of legitimate political concerns.

The 1967 war and its aftermath had major implications for gender roles and gender relations in Israel; it resulted in the reassertion and indeed celebration of militarized masculinity. To use Rein's words: "1967—and the June war of that year was for Israeli manhood the jewel in its crown of military achievement."[21] While ordinary Israeli-Jewish men were praised for their accomplishments on the battlefield, Israel's male elite leadership secured its unchallenged position at the center of Israeli-Jewish collectivity. Most women, on the other hand, had no direct part in the glory because they did not take part in the actual fighting. Their contributions on the homefront were either overlooked or taken for granted, viewed merely as the fulfillment of their assigned responsibilities as women.

It would be an understatement to say that the political climate in Israel in the aftermath of the 1967 war was far from encouraging alternative interpretations of the war—especially if they came from women. Most felt that Israel had no other choice but to wage war to defend its existence and that the price some people had to pay to reach that goal was inevitable. The largely unchallenged acceptance of this questionable interpretation silenced the few voices of dissent on the margins of the Israeli political spectrum and made the emergence of an anti-war or pro-peace movement almost impossible.

The few attempts by women to organize as women around contemporary political issues during that period were in support of the prevailing public consensus. For example, on the eve of the 1967 war, a group of women nicknamed "The Merry Wives of Windsor," staged a public demonstration in Tel-Aviv, calling for the appointment of hawkish Moshe Dayan as minister of defense to insure the appropriate militaristic response to crisis. A few years later, in 1975, a less known effort was undertaken by the "Women of the First Circle," who demanded that the Israeli government state clearly that it would *not* withdraw from the Occupied Territories.[22]

In light of the political climate and given the hegemony of Israeli men in the political arena, the very fact that women formed exclusively-female political groups and issued public statements deserves attention. In other words, these examples could be examined in the context of the long struggle of women in Israel for voice and visibility in the public political arena. At the same time, we must distinguish between political initiatives that aim to uphold the status quo and those that are designed to challenge it. Both examples—the Merry Wives of Windsor and the Women of the First Circle—were clearly in support of the public consensus and the political status quo. The women who organized these early actions did not attempt to articulate any connections between social and political issues and the problems facing them as women. Instead, they invoked prevailing notions of femininity such as care and unconditional support for their men to justify their intervention in the political debate and made no attempt to challenge its underlying assumptions nor its gendered underpinnings. The political consensus both on the Arab-Israeli conflict and on gender relations remained intact.

This was the context in which Golda Meir was elected prime minister. Yet her term, which lasted from 1969 to 1973, did nothing to alter the prevailing gender inequalities in Israel. In fact, many Israeli feminists maintain that Meir's tenure was a setback in women's struggles for equality in Israel. Judith Buber Agassi points out that "though herself a 'strong woman' who had fought for her own chance to enter politics, Golda certainly was no feminist. She was a traditionalist concerning gender roles and she did nothing to facilitate the entry into or the advancement of other women in Israeli politics."[23] Influenced by stereotypical representations of the U.S. women's movement in the 1960s that fueled the backlash against feminism in Israel during the 1970s, Golda Meir referred to feminists as "those crazy women who burn their bras and go around all disheveled and hate men" or as women who think that "it's a misfortune to get pregnant and a disaster to bring children into the world."[24]

The prime minister's attitudes toward the women's movement and her popular image as an Israeli legend, not a "real" woman, set her apart from the movement and, in a sense, from most Israeli women. Not only did she not empower women to enter politics, she did not in any way challenge men's dominance in the political arena as well as in every other sphere of influence in Israeli society. Ironically, though her political career became a pretext for the assertions that Israeli women were equal to men, she herself did not escape traditional feminine stereotypes and sexist jokes. For example, she became known nationally and internationally as "the ablest man in the cabinet," a description coined by Ben Gurion to assure Israel and the rest of the world that, despite her gender, Meir was capable of the masculine task of leading the country and upholding the political and social consensus.[25]

The political consensus and the status quo concerning gender relations began to dissolve somewhat during the 1973 war. This war represented an anticlimactic turning point in the construction of Israeli collective identity. It has been inscribed in Israel's history and popular culture as a collective trauma. By threatening to change the expanded borders of 1967 and shattering the illusion of military invincibility, it re-invoked the image of the Jew-as-victim grounded in the defensive national ethos. To this day, more than twenty years later, many Israelis frustrated with their inability to rewrite the 1973 war as a victory are still searching for scapegoats in order to rid themselves of the burden of collective responsibility.[26]

Apart from having a significant effect on Israeli-Jewish collective identity, the 1973 war also triggered a public discussion on the gendered division of labor in Israeli society. The war lasted only a few weeks, but the massive mobilization of Israel's reserve units had a dramatic effect on Israeli society and economy, as well as on women. With most of the men in the labor force taken to the battlefront, it seemed, at least during the first few days, that the country stopped functioning. Untrained and unskilled, women were frustrated as they were not able to replace the mobilized men at the machines, in manufacturing, in agriculture, and behind the wheels of buses.[27] Moreover, attempts by women to volunteer for various tasks on the homefront were not welcome either. As Marcia Freedman points out, "during the first days of the war, teen-age boys and older men were mobilized to provide essential services. When women volunteered, they were turned away. We were asked to knit woolen hats and bake cakes for men at the front."[28]

There were a few volunteer jobs for women on the homefront. Freedman, for example, had the experience of being a "hostess" in a small hotel in Haifa which was turned into a rest home for the mentally and emotionally wounded: "We were asked to be 'hostesses'—to serve coffee, try to talk with patients, play *sheshbesh*, backgammon. We were to raise morale, to be a reminder of normalcy. All that was required of us was our womanhood. We were not expected to have any therapeutic skills."[29] In light of this very gendered experience and given the emergence of a distinct women's movement in Israel at the time, women, not just feminists, began to ask critical questions about their position in society.

Less than a year after the war, the feminist movement in Israel dedicated a special issue of its newsletter to the topic: women and war.[30]

The issue focused on what happened to the Israeli women during the war, offering a penetrating critique of gender relations in Israeli society. It chronicled the social and political marginalization of women during the war—and its distorted representation in the Israeli media—and included a critical examination of the economic loss to the Israeli economy due to failure to consider women's work potential seriously. Also discussed in this context were the situation of women in the Israeli military and the social and political implications of the war for different groups of women.

This was the first time that women, mostly feminists, tried to address the connections between gender differences and war from both a practical and a theoretical perspective. Pnina Krindel stressed that the distinctions between masculinity and femininity, which become more rigid in times of war, represent "socially imposed patterns, rather than people's free choice or biological nature."[31] She further argued that "since the distinction between 'fighters' and 'non-fighters' is based on gender, not on qualifications or preferences, it is conceivable that many women would want to go and fight while men will prefer to stay home."[32]

In another article in the same issue, Ester Eilam presented a rather different feminist interpretation of the connections between gender and war. Dealing more broadly with the relationship between war as an institution and the social construction of masculinity, Eilam argued that "war represents a 'masculine' value par excellence" and that "the myth of war is grounded in the idealization of 'masculine' values such as heroism and loyalty and contrasting them with qualities such as fear and weakness that are associated with women."[33] Eilam's critique of the relationship of masculinity and war raises difficult questions for those antiwar feminists who argue for equality within the prevailing order. Instead of asking for mere inclusion of women in the war system, she argued that the struggle for eradication of inequalities in power and privilege was in fact an antiwar struggle.

These two different interpretations of the relationship between gender and war marked the beginning of an ongoing critical discussion around these issues in the feminist movement. Sparked by the 1973 war and culminating in the establishment of the Women's Party in 1977, this discussion represents an important new stage in the history of the Israeli women's movement.

The Emergence of a Feminist Movement (1970–1977)

The beginnings of the feminist movement in Israel is often traced to two seminars on women's issues taught at Haifa University in 1970 by Marcia Freedman and Marilyn Safir, both immigrants from the United States. These seminars evolved into consciousness-raising groups, generating considerable interest, and in less than two years spread to Tel-Aviv and Jerusalem, taking on a different character in each place. In Haifa, women established an organization they called *Nilahem*, which translates into "we will fight" and was also the acronym for Women for a Renewed Society. The group's mission statement presented a radical analysis of the causes and practices of the oppression of women in general and the male-dominated Israeli society in particular.[34]

The feminist organization in Tel Aviv on the other hand, which later became the Israel Feminist Movement, stressed legislative reform and political involvement in the social and political system as a means to achieve gender equality.[35] The Tel Aviv based movement could not have been more different than the independent feminist group that emerged in Jerusalem, comprised mostly of non-Zionist and anti-Zionist women activists. It stressed the need to eradicate not only gender oppression, but also that based on race, class, and national differences, and in addition it called for an end to the Israeli occupation of Palestinian lands.[36]

With the exception of the feminist group in Jerusalem, which had its origins in politically progressive social movements on the Israeli left, the women's movement in Israel, argues Barbara Swirski, "did not originate in a civil rights or student movement as it did in the United States and Western Europe, but was the result of the direct influence of new immigrants from the United States and other English speaking countries."[37] Unlike earlier attempts by Jewish women in the pre-state era to ground the ideals of gender equality in socialist Zionist ideology, the "new" women's movement was comprised primarily of middle-class, university-educated Ashkenazi women who did not, for the most part, seek a radical transformation of Israeli society. Rather, these women struggled for their equal place within the existing social and political structures in Israel.

Nevertheless, during the first years of their existence feminist groups undertook several important projects. In Haifa women examined and criticized discriminatory agendas in hiring practices at the Technion (the largest higher-education institution in Israel with a focus on the natural sciences), staged a demonstration to protest the implications of religious laws of marriage and divorce for women's lives, and conducted a successful campaign to persuade Haifa University to open a day-care center for students and employees. In other parts of the country, feminists set up women's centers, conducted extensive lecturing in schools, army bases and kibbutzim, supported striking nurses and social workers, held demonstrations for the liberalization of the abortion law, and embarked on feminist publishing ventures.[38]

The emerging women's movement was a social and political force that could no longer be ignored. Thus, when Shulamit Aloni formed the Citizen's Rights Movement (CRM) in 1973, she turned to the women's movement for help in gathering the number of signatures required to enter Israeli elections; in return, Marcia Freedman, as the representative of the women's movement, was allotted third place on the party slate. Although at the time of this alliance no one expected that Freedman would be elected, the women's movement still celebrated a victory because it's political power had finally been recognized. But contrary to most political analyses, as a result of the elections, the CRM won three seats in the Knesset, one of which belonged to Marcia Freedman, the outspoken feminist.[39]

Given the political climate in Israel at the time, this was indeed a great accomplishment for the feminist movement. Before the 1973 war, domestic issues had been expected to dominate the elections campaign initially scheduled for October 1973. In the aftermath, however, the campaign was overshadowed by political feuds and questions arising directly or indirectly from the war. Moreover, all major parties had fielded army officers among their candidates. The debate over national security had once again put domestic social issues, including gender issues and women's concerns, on the backburner. In this context, the CRM was the only party that "tried to fight the elections on issues close to the hearts of the people and brought a feminist on to its list."[40] The CRM focus on important domestic issues that had been neglected for so long was no doubt a factor in the CRM's popularity and unexpected strong showing in the elections. Yet, despite their success, their commitment to the feminist movement began to erode after the elections.[41]

Despite the lack of support within her own party and the hostile reaction toward her in the male-dominated Knesset, Marcia Freedman fought relentlessly during her term (1973–77) to raise awareness of gender discrimination and to initiate and push through legislations sensitive to women's needs and designed to improve their condition in society. What made Freedman particularly unpopular in the Knesset, and to a great extent even in the women's movement at the time, was the fact that in addition to speaking up about women's issues she took issue with oppression and discrimination experienced by other disenfranchised groups, including Palestinians in the Occupied Territories. In 1976, following the killing of three Palestinians by Israeli soldiers during a demonstration in the West Bank, Freedman spoke critically and with passion against Israeli torture of Palestinian political prisoners and the unchecked vigilante settler violence and in favor of the Palestinians' right to self-determination.[42]

Freedman's unequivocal positions on the Israeli-Palestinian conflict which clearly challenged the political consensus, led to an important debate in the feminist movement on the relationship between feminist politics and peace and security. The movement was forced to address the conflict which had been kept off the agenda until then. These debates inspired the first attempts to articulate linkages between the problems facing women in Israel and the issues of war, peace, and the Israeli occupation, and gave impetus to the establishment of the Women's Party in 1977.

Peace as a Women's Issue: The Women's Party (1977)

When Marcia Freedman's term ended in 1977, she led the effort to establish a Women's Party to run in the 1977 elections. The party provided a framework for the exploration and public articulation of linkages between women's issues and other social and political problems. In particular, it called attention to existing connections between different forms of oppression and between gender inequalities and the politics of the Arab-Israeli conflict. Its official election platform called for "gender equality [and] economic, political and social equality between people, men or women," as well as for "the abolition of existing structures of discrimination and gaps on the grounds of gender, ethnicity, nationality, age, ability or opinion."[43] These ideas, which had rarely been articulated in the Israeli political arena, were met with a nearly uniform hostile reaction.

Another connection that the Women's Party made which was unprecedented at the time and remains yet unaddressed in Israeli politics was to point out that the huge military budget comes at the expense of needed resource allocations for social programs and domestic issues. The platform stated that "the existing political situation consumes most of the Israeli society's resources and diverts the people's and government's attention away from crucial social problems."[44] The solution to these problems according to the Women's Party depended upon "the achievement of a comprehensive long lasting peace in the region [which] is inseparable from the establishment of an egalitarian society."[45] The platform clearly affirmed that it would "support any initiative that will lead to the resolution of the Arab-Israeli conflict while recognizing the Palestinian people's rights for self-determination and the safe existence of the state of Israel."[46]

Not only were such connections unpopular in the Israeli political climate during that time, they were often perceived as traitorous and as a threat to national security.[47] The suggestion that women's liberation was connected to the liberation of others, including Palestinians who lived under Israeli occupation, called into question the hegemonic discourse of national security which was predicated upon the continued occupation of Arab lands and thus, continued militaristic, masculinized definitions of national priorities. It also challenged the rigid distinction between "us" and "them" that was understood in terms of Jews and Arabs. The message of the Women's Party was explicit and clear: "We see Arab women within Israel and across the borders as sisters in a joint struggle for equal rights and equal opportunities and we wait for the day when we will be able to shake hands across national boundaries."[48]

Referring to Arab women as "sisters in a joint struggle" at that time was equivalent to political suicide. The majority of Israeli society was not ready to listen to the principled positions of women who sought to explore the connections between their own oppression and the oppression of others. As a result, the Women's Party did not win enough votes for a seat in Knesset and disbanded immediately after the elections. Despite this, many Israeli feminists regard the establishment of the party, and its participation in the 1977 elections, as an important milestone in the history of women's political activism in Israel.[49]

Women and the Politics of Change (1977–1982)

The most dramatic changes affecting Israeli women's lives and struggles prior to 1977 were related to the escalation of the Arab-Israeli conflict mostly through warfare and preparations for war. The 1977 elections and their aftermath introduced changes of a different sort, although they were still connected to the politics of war and peace in the region. Among those changes were the victory of the right-wing Likud party in the 1977 elections after twenty-nine years of Labor-led governments in Israel, the founding of an extra-parliamentary pressure group called Peace Now, and the signing of the Camp David Accords between Israel and Egypt.

The women's movement, however, continued its work on women's rights and equality as if nothing had changed within the broader sociopolitical context. None of the significant political changes nor their possible implications for women's lives in Israel was on the agenda of the first feminist conference, held in 1978 in Beer Sheba and attended by about 150 women. This may be attributed in part to the feelings of feminists who associated the failure of the Women's Party in the 1977 elections with the radical connections it made between women's issues and the politics of the Arab-Israeli conflict. Evidently, there was a fear among feminists that a further discussion of national and international politics would divert attention from women's issues and result in a further fragmentation of the already fragile movement. With the Israeli invasion of Lebanon in 1982, however, the women's movement could no longer ignore the broader political picture.

The Israeli Invasion of Lebanon and its Aftermath: Women Voice Dissent (1982–1987)

The 1982 Israeli invasion of Lebanon gave rise to the first example of Israeli women organizing explicitly against war. It also marked a turning point for the Israeli peace movement as a whole, sparking the emergence of a distinctive peace movement in Israel.[50] Peace Now—founded in 1978 by a group of Israeli reserve officers and soldiers who were not convinced that the government was doing enough to bring about peace with Egypt—situated itself at the center of the emerging Israeli peace movement through its superior resources and its ability to define peace as an issue of national security. Some Israeli women, on the other hand, searched for different peace frameworks and new strategies of resistance and activism against the war.[51]

Two major women's protest groups emerged during that period: Women Against the Invasion of Lebanon and Parents Against Silence. Both groups opposed the Israeli invasion of Lebanon and demanded an immediate withdrawal of Israeli forces from Lebanon. The groups differed, however, not only in their origins and in the positions they articulated against the war but also in the different strategies they used to achieve goals—particularly in the ways they linked (or did not link) their gender identity with their political positions.

The establishment of Parents Against Silence a year after the invasion was triggered by a letter to the editor published in the Israeli daily *Ha'aretz*. Shoshana Shmueli, a teacher and a mother of two, wrote the letter with a message that appealed to mothers' and fathers' sense of responsibility for their children fighting the war. She urged those with similar sentiments and concerns "to cease to be silent, to protest against those who bear the responsibility for this cursed war . . . and not to relinquish the struggle until our sons come home."[52] A week after the publication of the letter, Shmueli convened the first meeting of Parents Against Silence.

The group was comprised of between forty and fifty women (and a few men who gave support primarily behind the scenes). The organization maintained a high level of activity for two years. Its scope included holding demonstrations and protest rallies, publishing proclamations, issuing press releases, distributing stickers and explanatory material at supermarkets, beaches, and demonstrations, and collecting signatures on petitions. Major protest rallies were held near the prime minister's office in Jerusalem, in one of Tel Aviv's main squares, and near the ministry of defense in Tel Aviv.[53]

The members of Parents Against Silence, which the media and the Israeli public called Mothers Against Silence, publicly disassociated themselves from feminism and tried to project an image that would not be threatening to most Israelis. They insisted that they were simply mothers (and fathers) who were worried about their sons in combat.[54] On the other hand, Women Against the Invasion of Lebanon, was made up of women who had been active in the Israeli feminist movement and articulated their opposition to the war in the form of a feminist anti-militarist position. They stressed the connections between their oppression as women and other forms of oppression and domination suffered by Palestinians as a result of Israeli military occupation both in Lebanon and in the West Bank and Gaza Strip.

Israeli society and its mainstream media were sympathetic to Parents Against Silence, but did not tolerate the feminist antiwar and antioccupation positions articulated by Women Against the Invasion of Lebanon. Gadi Wolfsfeld points out that "unlike the feminist group, Parents Against Silence were pictured as mainstream Israel: mothers worrying about their sons in combat. To oppose the group politically was equivalent to insulting motherhood and the army at the same time."[55] The hostile public reaction toward Women Against the Invasion of Lebanon, however, revealed that Israeli society was not able to address the oppression of Palestinians in the Occupied Territories nor the subordination of Israeli women, and especially not the links between the two.

Parents Against Silence dispersed soon after the Israeli army pulled out of most of Lebanon in 1985. The active women in the group did not join feminist groups or other political organizations. Women Against the Invasion of Lebanon, on the other hand, changed its name to Women Against the Occupation (WAO) and expanded its antiwar focus to include solidarity campaigns with Palestinian women in the West Bank and Gaza Strip.[56]

In sum, the Israeli invasion of Lebanon in June 1982 triggered for the first time massive antiwar protests in Israel and galvanized a peace movement. Yet women had little room to challenge as women, let alone as feminists, the dominant rhetoric of national security, which prescribed the ideological notion of an Israeli woman who backs her sons and on occasion, only in the name of care and protection, may question government policies. Feminism was viewed as an extreme movement that posed a threat to the stability of Israeli society, particularly in times of crisis. This crisis atmosphere helped generate public hostility toward Women Against the Invasion of Lebanon in contrast to the empathetic attitude toward Parents Against Silence.

The women who founded Parents Against Silence stressed time and again that they were not feminists but rather mothers concerned with their sons on the battlefield. Such a position might have been a strategic decision designed to mobilize broad support for their cause without having to confront the dominant political discourse in Israel, but this does not appear likely in this particular case. What remains significant, however, is the centrality of the discourse of motherhood for women's peace activism in Israel and its broader legitimacy within Israeli society.

Despite the insistence of Parents Against Silence that their group included both mothers and fathers, the media and the public consistently called the group Mothers Against Silence. This indicates that the "task" of care, in Israel as in other places, is associated primarily with the experience of mothering and, as such, seriously limits social and political movements seeking a radical transformation of the prevailing political and social order including gender relations. Only with the outbreak of the *intifada*, has feminism gained some prominence among women peace activists in Israel.

7

Israeli-Jewish Women and the Intifada

➡ The outbreak of the *intifada* was a watershed for the political involvement of women in Israel. Exclusively female (and largely feminist)
peace groups burst on the scene, initiating activities that had two major goals: to mobilize public opinion in Israel and abroad against the
occupation and to build bridges of solidarity with Palestinian women
in the West Bank and Gaza Strip. Groups such as Women in Black,
the Women's Organizations for Women Political Prisoners (WOFPP),
the Israeli Women Against the Occupation (SHANI), the Women and
Peace Coalition, and the Israeli Women's Peace Net (RESHET), provided new frameworks for the political mobilization and activism of
women in Israel. These newly founded women's peace groups initiated
numerous demonstrations, letter campaigns, local and international peace
conferences, and solidarity visits to the West Bank and Gaza Strip.[1]

The mobilization of women's peace groups and their large scale
activism occurred long before already-existing organizations, such as
Peace Now, had taken unequivocal positions vis-à-vis the *intifada* and
against the Occupation—surprising to many, because Peace Now has
been the most widely recognized peace group, both in Israel and abroad.
For the most part, however, Peace Now has rarely moved beyond the
national consensus on the Palestinian question.[2] Although it organized
a number of demonstrations protesting Israeli government policy in the
Occupied Territories and calling for a negotiated solution to the conflict, Peace Now remained very cautious in its response to the *intifada*.
For example, it took the organization nearly a year to state that it was
in favor of direct negotiations between Israel and the PLO.[3]

The *intifada* caught the majority of Israeli society by surprise. Prior to that, information about the policies and practices used by the Israeli military in the Occupied Territories had often been subjected to both government and self-imposed media censorship.[4] During the early months of the uprising, however, as never before, the Israeli media broadcasted images and stories of life under occupation exposing some of the methods used by the Israeli military to suppress the po pular revolt. Most Israelis knew what was happening, although many acted as if they did not. Their initial responses reflected a mix of passivity and denial; confronting their images as brutal occupiers was too disturbing and too painful. It was women, in small groups at first, who confronted these images and grasped the message that ending the Occupation was the primary issue and challenged the general climate of passivity and denial within Israeli society.

The emergence of a multitude of women's peace groups provided women with new opportunities to step out of their prevailing roles as mothers and keepers of the homefront and to take positions on the most crucial matter in Israeli politics: the Israeli-Palestinian conflict. In this context, Israeli women have gradually come to realize that the broad array of concern and problems previously defined as "women's issues" cannot be treated anymore in isolation without reference to broader structures of militarization, inequality, and oppression reinforced by the Occupation.

Women Take Action:
The Emergence of a Women's Peace Movement (1987–1990)

The first reactions by women in Israel to the *intifada* were spontaneous, involving primarily those who had been previously active in either the Israeli left or the feminist movement or both. Acting within existing frameworks and channels, these women explored various ideas and strategies to educate the Israeli public about the *intifada*. In January 1988, a few weeks after the outbreak of the *intifada*, a group of women in West Jerusalem, members of a mixed-gender group, *Dai L'Kibbush* (Hebrew for End the Occupation), held a silent vigil under a banner bearing those words. This is how Women in Black in Jerusalem began. Hagar Rovlev, one of the seven women who organized the first vigil insists that its origins were largely experimental and that its success was highly contingent.[5] Nevertheless, the overwhelmingly supportive response by women to the idea led to its weekly institutionalization. In January 1988, women in Jerusalem, and soon thereafter throughout the country, began holding silent vigils on Friday afternoons. The women dressed in black to symbolize the tragedy of both Israeli and Palestinian peoples and held signs in Arabic, English, and Hebrew, which called for an end to the Israeli occupation of the West Bank and Gaza Strip.

Around the same time, women involved with the feminist magazine *Noga* collected slides taken by journalists in the Occupied Territories and installed a generator and a projector on a busy Tel Aviv street to show scenes from the West Bank and Gaza Strip that were prohibited by the Israeli military censor. Their main objective was to pierce the apathy and indifference of the average Israeli to the brutality of the Occupation.[6] According to *Noga* editor Rachel Ostrowitz who was part of the group, this particular initiative sprang out of "the need to understand what was happening in the West Bank and Gaza" and the realization "that censorship was being imposed on the public, and that television was not telling the whole story."[7]

Despite these strong convictions, hostile reactions of the Israeli public, and the logistical details required by this initiative, made the effort to show slides from the West Bank and Gaza Strip more and more difficult. Thus, soon after Women in Black in Jerusalem emerged, the women in Tel Aviv decided to substitute their slide show with a weekly vigil of Women in Black. They were also responsible for organizing the first unofficial delegation of forty Israeli-Jewish women, who attempted to visit refugee camps in the West Bank to see the situation for themselves and to express solidarity with Palestinian women. Although the group was stopped by the Israeli army before it reached its destination, this early initiative inspired numerous similar attempts, most of them successful.[8]

In Haifa, feminists and women who had been longtime activists on the Israeli left responded to the *intifada* by forming an ad hoc coalition that sponsored a number of meetings and demonstrations for International Women's Day in March 1988. This coalition was the driving force behind the Haifa-based Women in Black vigil.[9] In addition to the weekly vigils, Women in Black in Haifa also initiated a telegram

16. A Women in Black vigil. The Hebrew sign reads: "Talk Peace with the PLO." Tel Aviv, Israel, September 1990. *Courtesy Allan Clear, Impact Visuals.*

campaign addressed to the Israeli government and to military officials. The campaign which was carried out during the first two years of the *intifada* had two major objectives: to raise public awareness about the daily severity of the Israeli occupation and to express solidarity with Palestinians, especially with women.

Some telegrams protested the closure of Palestinian women's centers, the intimidation of women leaders in the West Bank and Gaza Strip, and the imprisonment of Palestinians without trials. Others demanded a supply of sanitary napkins for Palestinian women prisoners and improvement of prison conditions and medical care. The telegrams called attention to cases that were representative of the broader structure and practices of the Israeli occupation. Women in Black demanded explanations from both the Israeli government and the military for particular cases, naming the Palestinian women who were involved. In so doing, they challenged the dehumanizing practice of leaving Palestinians nameless.

In effect, the Palestinian women whose cases were mentioned were not presented as the enemy but rather as women whose suffering and resistance touched the lives of Israeli women who, in turn, made it part of their struggle to bring this information to the attention of the Israeli government, media, and public.[10]

Several other groups were founded around the same time, usually with a particular focus or project. In January 1988, women launched the Peace Quilt, a project to prepare a symbolic covering for a future negotiation table and to encourage dialogue between Palestinian and Jewish women in Israel. Made up of more than four thousand pieces of embroidery with messages of peace in Hebrew, Arabic, and English, it was assembled by Israeli-Jewish women and Palestinian women holding Israeli citizenship. The quilt was exhibited in front of the Knesset on June 5, 1988, in a protest vigil that marked the twenty-first anniversary of the Israeli occupation of the West Bank and Gaza Strip.

In addition to consistent protests against the occupation, women also began to address the implications of the occupation for women's lives. The WOFPP in Tel-Aviv and Jerusalem emerged soon after the outbreak of the *intifada* to confront the harassment and political detention of Palestinian women—aimed at inhibiting the vital function of women's organizations for the embattled Palestinian community. The Tel Aviv- and Jerusalem-based groups have functioned separately, although the scope of their activities has been similar, including public protests and legal intervention on behalf of Palestinian women around such issues as sexual harassment, assaults, and torture of Palestinian women prisoners as well as inappropriate jail conditions.[11]

WOFPP's main objective has been to support women political prisoners by challenging policies that violate their basic civil and human rights. The group has mobilized public opinion through press releases and demonstrations, put pressure on members of the Israeli parliament, public institutions, and local and international organizations, and has kept in close contact with the prisoners, their lawyers, and their families. In addition, clothing and other necessities are delivered to prisoners and solidarity visits are made to Palestinian women's houses after their release.

A great part of these groups' work consists of daily advocacy in the jails and in the detention centers where Palestinian women are held. In many cases, WOFPP members have served as go-betweens, or as unofficial mediators, between Palestinian families and the Israeli

17. An encounter between Intisar al-Quq, a former Palestinian woman prisoner (left) and Michal Schwartz, an Israeli woman activist from the Jerusalem-based group Women for Women Political Prisoners (right) during a solidarity visit of the group following Intisar al-Quq's release from three years of imprisonment in Israeli jails. Silwan (near East Jerusalem), Occupied West Bank, October 1992. *Courtesy Hilary Marcus, Impact Visuals.*

authorities.[12] Both the Tel Aviv and the Jerusalem group publish monthly newsletters and occasional reports featuring information about living conditions in the prisons as well as updates on recent imprisonments and trials—occasionally accompanied by photos of Palestinian women and their families.[13] In the context of Israeli society, where a great deal is invested in portraying Palestinians as uncivilized "others" and as vicious enemies of the state, attempts such as WOFPP's to put a human face on the victims of Israel's policies have been perceived as threats to Israeli national security.

As a result, there has been a tendency on the part of many Israelis to treat such activities as acts of national treason. Symptomatically,

WOFPP members have been often called "Arab-lovers" by Israeli policemen who guard the jails and prevented them from delivering necessary items such as soap, shampoo, sheets, towels, and sanitary napkins, which are not supplied by the prison authorities. The perception of solidarity work as an act of treason has also resulted in frequent prevention of WOFPP's lawyers from meeting with their Palestinian clients.[14]

In order to transform the hostile public climate in which women peace activists were operating and broaden their base of support, a number of women in Jerusalem who were either active in or supportive of both Women and Black and WOFPP established in 1988 a new group—SHANI, also known as Israeli Women Against the Occupation.[15] SHANI's analysis of the Israeli-Palestinian conflict and the prospects for its resolution contended that "women in every society tend to try and resolve conflicts peacefully before they turn to aggressive ways. We find it easier than men to express our willingness to compromise since we understand that peace has a price."[16]

To provide women more possibilities with which to form their perspectives on Middle East politics, the group organized symposia and discussions on different topics related to the conflict and invited Palestinian and Israeli speakers to present their views in public meetings held every three weeks. During the first three years of the *intifada*, SHANI attracted some two hundred women—many previously on the left or in the women's movement and others drawn into political work by the outbreak of the Palestinian uprising. In addition to its educational work, the group visited hospitals, schools, and kindergartens in the West Bank and Gaza Strip and helped organize and coordinate numerous protests and demonstrations with other groups in the Israeli women's peace movement. One of its major projects was a campaign to re-open schools and universities in the Occupied Territories launched in collaboration with Palestinian women and with various groups of Israeli and Palestinian educators.[17] SHANI also organized a signature collection campaign to endorse a document, known as the "Brussels Declaration," written and signed by Palestinian and Israeli women who participated in the first international women's peace conference in Brussels in May 1989.[18]

Participation in and support of women's peace conferences were central to the work of all the newly founded women's peace groups and to that of feminists and peace activists not affiliated with any particular group.[19] Prior to Brussels, on the first anniversary of the *intifada*, a coalition of women's peace groups in Israel organized a conference under the title: "Occupation or Peace: A Feminist Perspective." The meeting brought together several hundred Jewish and Palestinian women from Israel and representatives of the Palestinian women's committees from the West Bank and Gaza Strip. All the speakers made explicit connections between women's struggles for liberation and equality and the Palestinian struggles for national liberation and self-determination. Another set of connections made explicit was that between the violence of war and occupation and violence against women. The conference called for the establishment of an international committee for further action and urged women to step up their efforts to end of the occupation and to find a peaceful resolution of the Israeli-Palestinian conflict.[20]

To facilitate the implementation of the conference's conclusions, women founded an umbrella organization—Women and Peace—whose goals were to coordinate between the various women's peace groups in Israel and to communicate on a regular basis with Palestinian women's groups in the West Bank and Gaza Strip. In addition to the practical functions of networking and coordination, the Women and Peace was designed "to form a forceful political voice [of women] in Israeli society."[21] Its founding members insisted that "because women in Israel are not well represented in political institutions or in decision-making bodies, the organization of women outside the establishment is of great importance."[22] They believed that a broad coalition of women working for peace will make women's peace activism more visible and create more opportunities for their voices to be heard. In addition, some hoped that the newly founded coalition would make explicit attempts to influence government policies on the Israeli-Palestinian conflict.[23]

The first international women's peace conference on the Israeli-Palestinian conflict, titled "Give Peace a Chance—Women Speak Out" took place in May 1989 in Brussels. About fifty women from Israel and from the West Bank and Gaza Strip, met for the first time in a format that included women representatives of the PLO to discuss the Israeli-Palestinian conflict and the prospects for its resolution. At the conclusion of the conference, the participants drew up a document, affirming their commitment to a peaceful resolution of the conflict based on the recognition of the rights of all peoples in the region to live in dignity and security, the right of the Palestinian People to self-determination alongside Israel, and the right of all the sides to choose their legitimate representatives.[24]

Upon their return from Brussels, the Israeli participants formed the Israel Women's Peace Net (RESHET) which expanded to include thousands of members throughout Israel, with active branches in Jerusalem, Tel Aviv, Haifa and the Negev.[25] RESHET sought to expand the ranks of the women's peace movement to include more women from the political mainstream. Its activities were mainly educational in scope designed to transform people's positions on the Israeli-Palestinian conflict; only occasionally was it involved in protest actions. Unlike other women's peace groups that operate mainly on the grassroots, the leadership of RESHET is made up of well-known women, the majority of whom are part of the political establishment of the Zionist center and left in Israel, namely the Labor party and the coalition party MERETZ.[26]

On the second anniversary of the *intifada*, in December 1989, Israeli women organized a day of discussions and protest in Jerusalem under the title: "Women Go for Peace." They began in West Jerusalem with a conference organized and hosted by the Israeli Women and Peace Coalition where Palestinian women activists from the Occupied Territories were also invited to speak. Speakers at the conference situated the phenomenon of women's peace activism in Israel in an international context, pointing to other examples of women's struggles for peace such as the Madres de Plaza de Mayo in Argentina, the Black Sash in South Africa, and the women of Greenham Common in England.[27]

For the first time, Israeli women articulated fairly explicit and elaborate critiques of the connection between militarism and sexism, with numerous references to the connection between the oppression of Israeli women and the oppression of Palestinians in the West Bank and Gaza Strip. The conference was followed by a Women in Black demonstration—culminating in a march from West to East Jerusalem, where it was joined by Palestinian women—and ended in the Palestinian Al-Hakawati theatre with six thousand women participating. The last event of the day was an afternoon conference organized and hosted by Palestinian women to which Israeli women were invited.[28]

The unprecedented number of women's peace groups in Israel that emerged in response to the *intifada* created new frameworks through which many Israeli women have tried to come to terms with the connections between problems facing them as women and the broader sociopolitical context largely shaped by the Israeli-Palestinian conflict. Yet, the Israeli women's peace movement has thus far failed to become relevant to the majority of women in Israel. This is reflected both in its composition and in its agenda. The demographic profile of the movement resembles those of other women's movements and peace movements in Europe and in North America that are often accused of being elitist; it is comprised of women who are predominantly Ashkenazi, middle-class with formal academic education.[29]

The particular ethnic and class composition of the movement and the fact that it did not make the struggle against the glaring inequalities between Ashkenazi and Middle Eastern Jews and between Jews and Palestinians in Israel part of its agenda have contributed to its inability to relate to the concerns of the majority of Israeli women. According to Katia Azoulay "the 'typical Jewish woman' . . . is unrepresented in . . . and snubbed by the academics and other professionals in the 'women's peace movement,' who see her as shallow and simple-minded, and therefore, unworthy of cooption into their ranks."[30] Azoulay urges the Israeli women's peace movement to make its message and activities more relevant to the majority of women in Israel.

The growing awareness among Israeli women peace activists of the explicit and implicit ways in which gender and the politics of the Israeli-Palestinian conflict are interwoven and affect every facet of their lives may be an important step toward a more comprehensive and more inclusive analysis that will broaden the movement's agenda and in turn change its composition.[31]

Making the Links:
Gender and the Israeli-Palestinian Conflict

There are several sets of connections that Israeli women peace activists have stressed: (1) between different systems of domination and structured inequalities grounded in disparities of power and privilege; (2) between practices of violence used against Palestinians in the West Bank and Gaza Strip and the increase in violence against women in Israel; and (3) between struggles of Palestinians in the Occupied

Territories and women in Israel for liberation and self-determination. Taken together, these connections have formed the basis for new perspectives on the Israeli-Palestinian conflict articulated by women peace activists in Israel.[32]

But as feminist peace activist Rachel Ostrowitz suggests, "the connection women make between peace and their own lives is not surprising."[33] Ostrowitz believes that the similarities between the treatment of both Palestinians and women, within the context of the conflict, have helped women recognize that women's "marginality is not acceptable nor is the oppression of others."[34] To illustrate "the similarity in the treatment of oppressed human beings," Ostrowitz points out, for example, the similarity in media coverage of Palestinians, who have died at the hands of the Israeli military during the *intifada* and of women in Israel, who have suffered violence at the hands of Israeli men; both Palestinians and women "are often treated as persons without names."[35] These omissions help legitimize their daily discrimination and humiliation.

Ostrowitz also delineates the relationship between violence against Palestinians in the West Bank and Gaza Strip and the steep increase in violence against women on the Israeli homefront. She points out that "a soldier who serves in the West Bank and Gaza Strip and learns that it is permissible to use violence against other people is likely to bring that violence back with him, upon his return to his community," and that this spillover has direct implications for women's lives in Israel.[36] The story of Gilad Shemen further underscores this argument.

Gilad Shemen is a twenty-three-year old Israeli-Jewish man, who in April 1989, during his military service in Gaza, shot and killed a seventeen-year-old Palestinian woman, Amal Mohammad Hasin, as she was reading a book on her front porch. The regional military court convicted Shemen of carelessness in causing Hasin's death, but he was released after an appeal. Two years later, on June 30, 1991, Shemen shot and killed his former girlfriend, nineteen-year-old Einav Rogel. He was sent for mental health evaluation and serves a reduced sentence in an Israeli jail. Feminists peace activists in Israel have argued that the perverse connection between the two women's murders is but one symptom of the strong link between militarism and sexism in Israel.[37] This interpretation, however, was conspicuously missing from most accounts of the case in the mainstream Israeli media. Israeli journalist Gabi Nizan was among the few who did address the connections between the two murders. A few days after Rogel's murder, he wrote in the mass circulation newspaper *Hadashot*: "in a country without wars, Einav Rogel and Amal Mohammad Hasin could have been good friends. In such a world Gilad Shemen could have been a good friend of both of them. But in our society, Shemen met both of them with a gun in his hand. This is very normal for an Israeli man his age."[38]

Another topic omitted in most accounts of the *intifada* involves the sexual harassment and sexual violence inflicted upon Palestinian women prisoners. Since the beginning of the uprising, the WOFPP has received numerous complaints of sexual violence committed by Israeli military forces against Palestinian women. Such incidents occur not only during interrogation but also in the context of street patrols and the suppression of demonstrations. The case of thirty-six-year-old Fatma Abu Bacra from Gaza, arrested in November 1986, illustrates the sexual abuse and humiliation to which Palestinian women have been subjected during interrogation by the Israeli Security Services and throughout their imprisonment.

In the course of systematic pressure put on Abu Bacra to confess, one Israeli interrogator touched her face and breast, while another showed her a picture of a naked man and told her that the picture was of himself. He then took off his clothes and threatened to rape her if she did not sign the confession prepared by the military, which she refused to do. Later, she was removed by one of her interrogators to a separate room, with no policewoman present (in violation of regulations), and forced to sit in a corner with her head wedged between the interrogator's legs while he touched her, verbally abused her, threatened her with rape if she did not confess, and eventually masturbated to sexual climax in her presence. After this, Abu Bacra finally yielded to the pressure and signed the confession. On November 22, 1988, her detailed affidavit was submitted to a military judge by her lawyer, a member of the WOFPP, as the basis for a pretrial hearing on the validity of admissions Abu Bacra had made under torture. Nevertheless, to keep the issue of sexual violence off the agenda of the military courts, she was offered a plea bargain, which because of her deteriorating health and her two small children, she could not refuse.[39]

In addition to the connections between the violence against Palestinians in the Occupied Territories and violence against women,

Israeli feminists have criticized the priorities of state structures and institutions that view land as more important than people's lives and invest in military equipment instead of in securing equal pay for women or better education for children.[40] Dalia Sachs, a founding member of Women in Black in Haifa, argues that the practices of occupation are closely interlinked with the prevailing order within Israeli society.[41] For Sachs, "the occupation with its oppressive policies is a particular manifestation of the patriarchal, sexist, racist and militaristic society in which we live."[42] In particular, she points to the linkages between the policies and practices "of oppression, discrimination, exploitation by the Israeli-Jewish (Ashkenazi ruled) government not only of Palestinians in the West Bank and Gaza Strip, but also of women and other disadvantaged populations within Israel."[43]

What these sets of connections reveal is that all issues, including local and international politics, are *women's issues* and conversely that *women's issues* are in fact political issues of the most fundamental kind. In other words, by articulating such linkages, women peace activists have called into question the artificial distinctions between "public" and "private" and between narrowly defined "women's issues" and "politics." For the first time in the history of the women's movement in Israel, the feminist conviction that "the personal is political" has been infused with new meanings, opening new possibilities for social and political mobilizing.

As a result, attempts by women peace activists to link their struggles to end the Israeli occupation of the West Bank and Gaza Strip with their efforts to eradicate gender discrimination, and other structured inequalities and disparities in power and privilege within Israel, have been met with great resistance on the Israeli streets. These connections are resisted, silenced, or marginalized because they upset the status quo of contemporary Israeli society, culture, and politics and challenge the way in which the perennial appeal to national security actually serves to silence critical questions about the political composition and content of the "nation" whose security is said to be threatened. By pointing to the daily insecurities faced by different social groups within Israeli society, not to mention those under its direct military control, these connections challenge those who benefit most from defining the nation and security in narrow, militaristic, and male-dominated terms predicated upon the continued occupation of people's land.

Given the pervasiveness of this very particular interpretation of security, which places the security of the nation above that of its citizens, it is not surprising that the majority of Israelis have continued to resist and discredit issues that women peace activists have raised. Israeli women's campaigns to end the Occupation and to articulate alternative frameworks for peace, as well as their collaboration with Palestinian women in the West Bank and Gaza Strip, have not been taken seriously by Israeli politicians, nor by the state-controlled Israeli media. In addition, women's peace initiatives, especially Women in Black, have become favorite targets for verbal and physical violence that is almost always laced with sexual and sexist innuendoes. As with earlier cases of women's activism, such as the Women's Party and Women Against the War in Lebanon, the backlash against women peace activists has been fueled by a normally concealed discourse of national security that has institutionalized a belief that the political mobilization of women against government policies represents a social and political threat to the active social order itself.

The threat is twofold: Women challenge their socially assigned roles by stepping into the public-political arena and taking a position on the Israeli-Palestinian conflict—which is considered to be the most important matter in Israeli politics. And their position stands in opposition to the national consensus and disrupts prevailing understandings of womanhood and manhood in Israeli society. By trying to keep women's perspectives out of the official political debate in Israel, and by silencing women's voices of dissent at the grassroots level through the use of sexually loaded terminology and threats of physical intimidation, many Israeli men have expressed their fears, frustrations, and inability to cope with the new conceptions of womanhood forged by women peace activists in Israel. These systematic attempts to silence women's voices and to marginalize their struggle were unsuccessful until the outbreak of the Gulf War.

Silenced by War:
Women's Peace Activism and the Gulf War

Despite attempts by the Israeli government to use the Gulf crisis—following the Iraqi invasion of Kuwait and the massive U.S.

18. A man from the Israeli Right-wing party "Tsomet" demonstrating against
Women in Black during the Gulf crisis. The sign reads: "Women in Black for
Saddam." Tel Aviv, Israel, September 1990. *Courtesy Allan Clear, Impact
Visuals.*

military deployment in the Gulf—to divert attention from the *intifada*, the Israeli women's peace movement continued its activities until the start of the war on January 16, 1991. A press release published on September 6, 1990 by the Women and Peace Coalition, asserted that "women refuse to accept war as a solution to solve conflicts no matter how complicated they may be" and that "especially in this period of crisis there is a need to reinforce the belief in the principle of dialogue and the search for peaceful solutions."[44] More specifically, the statement pointed out that "the Persian Gulf Crisis and the danger of war reinforce the immediate need for negotiations with the legal representative of the Palestinians, the PLO, as the only way to reach a peaceful solution to the conflict and to prevent the horror of war."[45]

Despite this press release, which reaffirmed the commitment of the Israeli women's movement to a peaceful resolution of the Israeli-Palestinian conflict, when the U.S. bombing of Iraq started and Iraqi SCUD missiles were fired at Israel women's antiwar voices were not heard. To understand this unexpected silence, we must consider the fact that since the establishment of the state, it had become powerfully institutionalized for Israelis to forget their differences and form a united front when confronted with a direct threat or attack from the outside. Another factor making it difficult for women to affirm their antiwar positions was the pro-war position endorsed by the mainstream Israeli peace movement.

Israel's mainstream peace movement—identified with Peace Now and with the Zionist left parties, which are now part of the MERETZ bloc—supported the Gulf War with little equivocation. In fact, it appeared as if the peace movement saw the war as a pretext to return to the fold and find a common basis in support of the state. The only exceptions were a few groups on the margins of the movement such as the Alternative Information Center, Hanitzoz-Challenge, Israeli and Palestinian Physicians for Human Rights, and the WOFPP. These groups, who have had a long tradition of solidarity work with Palestinians in the West Bank and Gaza Strip, continued their work and at the same time tried to draw attention to the political interests behind the war and to the heavy price it would exert on the entire region.[46]

The women's peace movement, however, was not able to articulate a unanimous anti-war position. In fact, for the first time since the *intifada*, Women in Black suspended their weekly vigils. After intense debate, the vigils eventually resumed, though not in all locations and with limited participation.[47] The Gulf crisis also interrupted the planning of an international women's peace conference jointly organized by Palestinian and Israeli women and scheduled to take place in December 1990 in Jerusalem. As the level of repression against Palestinians increased with events such as the Haram-al-Sharif massacre in Jerusalem and long curfews that were imposed on the entire West Bank and Gaza Strip, joint planning meetings for the conference were postponed and never resumed in the same format. A modified version of the conference did take place, however, in December in West Jerusalem under the banner: "Women Struggle for Peace in a Time of Crisis." Although the conference featured a number of speeches by Palestinian women from the Occupied Territories, the vast majority of the participants were Jewish women from Israel and from abroad.[48]

In addition to its general impact on Israeli society, on the peace movement and on the women's movement, the Gulf War had particular implications for gender roles and gender relations in Israel. According to reports from battered women's shelters and rape crisis centers in Israel, there was a sharp increase in male violence against women and children during the war and in its aftermath. As a result, many more Israeli women began to address connections between the increase of violence against women and the politics of the Israeli-Palestinian conflict which served to legitimize the militarization of Israeli society.[49]

The Gulf War challenged for the first time the clear division of roles between men warriors and women caretakers. This time, unlike in all previous wars and emergency situations, Israeli men were not drafted into service. Men remained on the homefront, confronted with their families' fears, with their own fears, and with the vulnerability and helplessness of being locked in sealed rooms to protect themselves from the threat of gas attacks. The image of the invincible Israeli soldier, ready at all costs to protect women and children, was endangered. Israeli men became increasingly uncomfortable with this unfamiliar role; many used the word "impotent" to describe their feelings. Unable to express themselves violently against Arabs, as they were socialized and trained to do, many Israeli men "cured" their feelings of impotence and longings for the excitement of the battlefield by projecting their aggression onto women and children.[50]

Despite the crisis it prompted, the Gulf War represented a turning point for women's peace activism in Israel in that it triggered an

unprecedented public debate within the movement and, to some extent, in the society at large on the relationship between militarism and
violence against women. Nevertheless, attempts within the women's
peace movement to mobilize around these issues were soon derailed
with the appearance of the 1991 Madrid peace conference on the public
political scene. Before they were able to overcome the crisis of war,
women peace activists in Israel were confronted with a crisis of peace
prompted by new political developments in local, regional, and global
politics.

Silenced by Peace:
From Madrid to Oslo (1991–1993)

In the aftermath of the Gulf War, many women peace activists
in Israel tried to forget the contradictions and numbness in the movement during the war, but within a short while, they were confronted
by new challenges. The movement was unable to mobilize against the
massive deportations of 415 Palestinians, the blockade-style closure
imposed on the Occupied Territories, and the July 1993 Israeli attack
on Southern Lebanon. Many women peace activists felt reluctant to
criticize the national consensus on peace and security issues, especially
because MERETZ, the prominent representative of the Israeli left,
joined the Labor-led government. This reluctance, however, triggered
in many women feelings of frustration, burnout, and helplessness.

During the summer of 1993, almost six years after the start of the
intifada, the women's peace movement faced a major crisis. Women in
Black decreased from thirty-three to about twelve permanent vigils and
a few sporadic ones. Encounters with Palestinian women in the West
Bank and Gaza Strip were almost nonexistent, and the few that did take
place involved only Palestinian and Israeli-Jewish women who explicitly supported the peace overtures.[51] The crisis intensified significantly
following the dramatic announcement of the signing of the Israeli-
Palestinian Declaration of Principles in September. In its aftermath,
Women in Black in Jerusalem held several discussions to explore the implications of the new developments for their weekly vigil.[52]

Some Women in Black activists insisted that these developments
would cause a steady decline in the number of vigil participants, which
would gradually weaken the impact of the group; they suggested to end

the vigil before that happened. But most women were in favor of con-
tinuing the vigil while adding some sign to acknowledge the new
political situation. The decision at the conclusion of the meeting was
to provide a white sash saying "Yes to Peace" for any woman choosing
to wear it.[53] Nevertheless, on October 20, 1993, Women in Black ended
their weekly Friday vigil. The decision was a result of difficulty in reach-
ing a consensus on the future of the vigil in light of the apparent
contradiction between the strong uncompromising message of "End
the Occupation," and the celebratory mood of women who wanted to
hold a vigil in support of the peace process under the slogan "Yes to
Peace."[54]

Left open, however, was the possibility that if the current diplo-
matic attempts to find a solution to the Israeli-Palestinian conflict did
not measure up to expectations, Women in Black in Jerusalem would
resume their weekly vigil against the occupation. Indeed, there were
several attempts to resume the vigil. For example, on December 10,
1993, when it became apparent that the Israeli military would not begin its withdrawal from Gaza and Jericho on December 13, 104 Jerusalem Women in Black renewed their vigil with slogans supporting peace
and condemning settler violence.[55] A few months later, in June 1994,
Women in Black gathered once again, this time to mark twenty-seven
years of Israeli occupation. The weekly vigil, however, is not being held
anymore on a regular basis.[56]

There is no doubt that the crisis in the women's peace movement
has been prompted, among other things, by the change in government
from Likud to Labor and by the narrowing of political discussions to
statements for or against the Madrid peace process or for or against the
Gaza and Jericho First plan and the Declaration of Principles. Nevertheless, this crisis cannot be overcome by time or by a new catchy slogan around which most women peace activists will unite because it is
not only a crisis of direction and political strategy. Rather, it is first and
foremost an identity crisis. As such, it calls for a critical rethinking of
not only strategies of struggle, but also of the very basis of women's
organizing around questions of peace and security. The history of the
women's peace movement in Israel, like the histories of resistance
movements around the world, has been driven by attempts to overlook
differences in political ideology and direction in order to reach a broad
consensus designed to mobilize large segments of society.

19. A Women in Black vigil expressing support for the Gaza and Jericho First plan. West Jerusalem, Israel, January 1994. *Courtesy Alison Bradley, Impact Visuals.*

This search for a consensus in the women's peace movement has often suppressed differences—between women who joined Women in Black as mothers of sons who serve in the Occupied Territories and women who were strongly in favor of Israeli soldiers' refusal to serve in the West Bank and Gaza Strip and between women who joined the vigil because of the sexist nature of the Israeli peace movement and radical feminists whose participation in the vigil has been grounded in a principled position against any type of oppression. Other suppressed differences concern women's positions on feminism and Zionism and their perspectives on the long-term solution to the Israeli-Palestinian conflict.[57]

In addition to marginalizing differences within the movement, women peace activists have been reluctant to publicly address the connections between gender and the politics of the Israeli-Palestinian conflict, which are inherent in the structural underpinning and legitimization of the relationship between militarism and sexism and between violence against women in Israel and the violence and oppression of Palestinians in the Occupied Territories. Given the present political situation, the ability of women peace activists not only to overcome the present crisis but also to emerge as a politically significant force in Israel requires the courage to acknowledge and address these differences and uncomfortable connections.

The spontaneous large-scale political mobilization of women in Israel, during the first years of the *intifada,* confirms that Israeli women are ready and determined to struggle for a distinct voice and place within the peace movement and in the broader political arena in Israel. It would be a grave mistake, therefore, to interpret the inability of the women's peace movement to confront the unexpected political developments of the past two years as a sign of failure or burnout. Such an interpretation, which is common among women activists themselves, is indicative of the reactive nature of peace activism in Israel; the common view is that it is the task of grassroots activists to immediately respond to events unfolding in the official political arena. This limited understanding of resistance has narrowed the parameters of possible responses by the women's peace movement in Israel.

In conclusion, the present crisis presents women peace activists in Israel with a unique opportunity to rethink the dominant understandings of resistance and activism and to explore new venues to address the connections between gender and the Israeli-Palestinian conflict, that have affected their lives in powerful ways. Such an analysis, however, does not begin with the question of women's support of or opposition to war or peace, but rather focuses on their implications for women's lives and struggles on both sides of the Israeli-Palestinian divide.

8

The Politics of Alliances Between Palestinian and Israeli Women

➔ In addition to invigorating the Palestinian women's movement and triggering the emergence of a distinct women's peace movement in Israel, the *intifada* also created numerous opportunities for encounters and joint ventures between Israeli and Palestinian women. Prior to the uprising, planned meetings and political alliances between these groups were almost nonexistent; the few alliances that did exist were not based on gender but rather on shared positions on the Israeli-Palestinian conflict, and on personal relationships that evolved in the context of ongoing exchanges between Israeli peace activists who were mostly affiliated with non-Zionist and anti-Zionist groups and Palestinians affiliated with the factions of the PLO that had a progressive socialist platform—namely the DFLP, PFLP, and the communist party.

The relationship between Palestinian women in the West Bank and Gaza Strip and Israeli-Jewish women in Israel changed significantly during the first two years following the outbreak of the *intifada*. This chapter explores the origins and history of the relationship between the Palestinian women in the West Bank and Gaza Strip and Jewish women in Israel, focusing primarily on different types of alliances between these groups, especially since the beginning of the *intifada* in December 1987. The encounters of and fragile alliances between Palestinian and Israeli-Jewish women will be examined in relation to the historical trajectory of the Israeli-Palestinian conflict and its impact on particular political developments.

131

The History of Women's Alliances

The alliances between Palestinian and Israeli-Jewish women triggered by the *intifada* had historical precedents. Feminist historians and anthropologists examining the historic evolution of inter-communal relations in the region point out that various associations between women of different cultural, ethnic and religious communities existed long before the current stage of the Israeli-Palestinian conflict.[1] According to Elise Young "women's associations—formal and informal networks, acting autonomously or connected to wider political systems—have historically supported intercommunal relations among Jews, Muslims, and Christians in the Arab world."[2]

The often overlooked history of associations and alliances between Jewish, Muslim, and Christian women in the Middle East challenges both hegemonic narratives of the Israeli-Palestinian conflict and misogynist claims that women are natural enemies. At the same time, there has been a tendency to idealize alliances between women, especially if they represent opposing national collectivities, and to emphasize in particular their ability to transcend national boundaries.[3] According to this view, alliances between women have the potential to shape and redefine the boundaries of communities and intercommunal relations.

National movements, however, have placed, according to this view, major obstacles in the path of women's associations. Many feminist thinkers have drawn attention to the fact that nationalisms tend to reinforce the power and privilege of patriarchal institutions by forcing women to demonstrate their loyalty to these institutions and by turning them into symbols of their national collectivities.[4] At the same time, it is often national movements that trigger and inspire women's associations. Thus, we must recognize that Zionism and Palestinian nationalism have not always had such uniformly negative effects on women; multifaceted struggles of Arab and Jewish women in Palestine since the turn of the century gave rise to a complex relationship, between these two groups, involving both contingent alliances and serious conflicts and confrontations. The first attempts at alliance in the context of rising Jewish and Arab nationalisms can be found in the establishment of the League for Arab-Jewish Friendship in 1921 and in a number of alliances between Arab and Jewish women employed as factory workers.[5]

It was not uncommon for Jewish women, who emigrated to Palestine in the early 1900s, to connect their struggles for equal rights and equal pay to those of Arab workers. Women argued that "the discrepancy between the wages of women and men in the Jewish labor movement [was] comparable to the discrepancy between the wages of Arab workers and Jewish workers."[6] In February 1927, for example, sixty Jewish women and forty Arab women factory workers in Acre organized a joint strike in protest of low wages and intolerable working conditions.[7] But according to Elise Young, the Zionist leadership at the time "thwarted all attempts at solidarity between Arab and Jewish workers, fostering horizontal hostility among women."[8] As pressure mounted with the escalation of the Arab-Jewish conflict during the British Mandate, and particularly with the establishment of the state of Israel in 1948—which cemented the divisions between the two communities—alliances between Jewish and Palestinian women became very scarce.

As for the broader attempts to build bridges of understanding between Palestinians and Jews, it is not clear if any of them involved women. There is no reference to the participation of women in the bi-nationalist party, established in 1936 by Martin Buber, Judah Magnes, and Dr. Nissim Malul in an effort to reach a modus vivendi with the Palestinians, or in *Brith Shalom* (Covenant of Peace) and the *IHUD* (unity) Association, established in the twenties and forties respectively to foster cooperation between the Zionist and Arab nationalist movements. In addition to these efforts, there were several attempts by Jewish and Palestinian businessmen and civil leaders to ease tensions between the communities. Again, it is not clear, from the few accounts concerning these initiatives, how many women were part of these projects and what were their roles.[9]

Encounters and alliances between Israeli-Jewish and Palestinian women became particularly infrequent following the 1948 war and the establishment of the state of Israel. An exception was the Democratic Women's Movement (TANDI) founded in 1948 by Arab and Jewish women members of the Communist Party in Israel. TANDI's declared objectives were to work for women's rights, children's rights, and peace. The joint movement of Arab and Jewish women saw the struggle for women's equality as inseparable from the process of transforming Israel into a truly democratic society that would include full equality for the Arab population as well as for other groups, and a separation between religion and state. TANDI was the first women's group in Israel to celebrate International Women's Day with marches, demonstrations, and public events to stress the importance of both women's equality and Arab-Jewish solidarity.[10]

Apart from the work of TANDI, face-to face, organized encounters between Palestinian women in the Occupied Territories and Israeli-Jewish women in Israel were almost nonexistent prior to the outbreak of the *intifada*. The few sporadic attempts by Israeli-Jewish women to express in solidarity with Palestinian women in the West Bank and Gaza Strip remained unnoticed in Israel, but received some publicity in the Palestinian press. One such attempt involved a relatively small group of Israeli-Jewish women, Women Against the Occupation (WAO), formally known as Women Against the Invasion of Lebanon, that initiated different activities and projects designed to publicize the plight of Palestinian women prisoners.[11]

In March 1984, the group demonstrated outside the Neve Tirtza women's prison in solidarity with Palestinian women prisoners who went on a hunger strike to protest their ill treatment. When word was received that women prisoners were tear-gassed inside their cells, WAO demanded and received a Knesset investigation of the incident. Other activities included a women's march in Tel Aviv on International Women's Day, in 1984, to protest Palestinian women's prison conditions, as well as successful campaigns to release Leila Mer'i, a Birzeit University Student Council member, and to cancel the town arrest of Amal Wahdan, an activist in the PFWAC.[12]

Based on early examples of Israeli women's solidarity with Palestinian women prisoners, Palestinian scholar and activist Ghada Talhami concluded that "the record of Women Against the Occupation disproves the thesis that a Western-oriented feminist movement is incapable of empathizing with a Third World feminist movement."[13] At the same time, Talhami stressed that this was not the case with "other mainstream Israeli feminist organizations."[14] Indeed, it was not until the outbreak of the *intifada* that mainstream Israeli feminist organizations became interested in the lives and struggles of Palestinian women in the West Bank and Gaza Strip. In addition to invigorating the Palestinian women's movement, and triggering the emergence of a distinct women's peace movement in Israel, the *intifada* created better conditions for cooperation between women on opposite sides of the Israeli-

Palestinian divide. These conditions enabled an unprecedented number of different types of interactions in the shape of dialogue groups, local and international conferences, solidarity visits, joint demonstrations, and collaborative work on specific projects.[15]

Echoing the sentiments of many women peace activists in Israel, Israeli feminist Rachel Ostrowitz points to the *intifada* as the primary catalyst for the emergence of networks and connections involving both Palestinian and Israeli-Jewish women. Before the *intifada*, women in Israel "hardly had any contacts with Palestinian women inside Israel, let alone in the West Bank and Gaza Strip."[16] Israeli-Jewish women had been too busy with their own problems "to realize that even though Palestinian women face a reality that is different than ours and deal with different problems, there are things that we have in common and topics that we can and should discuss with one another."[17]

Many women peace activists in Israel have admitted that their own activism was prompted by the high visibility of Palestinian women's political involvement during the early stages of the *intifada*. Images of strong and defiant Palestinian women at the forefront of their struggle had an empowering effect on many Israeli-Jewish women. The massive mobilization of Palestinian women prompted a sense of commitment and solidarity grounded in the feminist vision of global sisterhood and in the realization that Palestinian women were ready and willing to talk peace and that this opportunity should not be missed.

The political agency, independence, and active participation of Palestinian women in the *intifada* called into question their stereotypical depictions as passive, subservient, dependent and confined to the home. The majority of Israeli women peace activists celebrated the "new" Palestinian woman with whom they felt an affinity, since she seemed more like them. They, however, did not engage in a critical examining of the processes and practices that have constructed the images of pre-*intifada* Palestinian women not only as essentially different but also as inferior to Israeli-Jewish women. The change in the images and roles of Palestinian women has been interpreted by many Israeli-Jewish women as well as by some North American and European feminists as a shift from "tradition" to "modernity." According to this interpretation, by enabling Palestinian women to transcend the confines of the private sphere and to enter the public-political arena, the *intifada* created better conditions for the emergence of alliances with their more "developed" sisters. In other words, the underlying assumption has been that successful alliances should be based on similarities and therefore that Palestinian women had to change and become more like Israeli-Jewish women.

Palestinian women, on the other hand, saw the *intifada* as an important catalyst that might disturb and thus transform the political positions of Jewish women in Israel and abroad. According to sociologist Nahla Abdo, "the *intifada* has registered a historic turn in the Israeli-Palestinian relationship as far as political alliances—no matter how symbolic—are concerned."[18] Focusing particularly on the impact of the *intifada* in general and of Palestinian women in particular on Jewish feminists, Abdo asserts that "the Palestinian women's movement has shaken up the Jewish feminist movement in Israel and abroad. Jewish feminists' silence, complicity and indifference to the struggle of Palestinians against the racist Israeli state is being broken down."[19] In conclusion, Abdo argues that "the politicization of some Jewish feminists circles in Israel (e.g., Women in Black and Women for Palestinian Women Political Prisoners) is the product of the Palestinian women's uprising."[20]

Although Palestinian and Jewish women share the view that the *intifada* transformed their relationship to one another, their interpretations of the nature of the relationship reflect different sets of expectations. Palestinian women had hoped the uprising would trigger a radical transformation in the political views of Israeli-Jewish women and would enable them to engage in solidarity work with Palestinians in the West Bank and Gaza Strip and to mobilize support against the Occupation within the Israeli society. They envisioned alliances based on the recognition that their relationship with Israeli-Jewish women is, first and foremost, that between occupiers and occupied. Thus, the transformation of the relationship depends on the willingness of Israeli-Jewish women to account for the ways in which they themselves are implicated in the structures and policies of the Israeli government and for the power and privilege they enjoy as Israeli citizens.

But many Israeli-Jewish women activists were not yet ready to meet these expectations. Although they were not only interested, but actually excited, about meeting Palestinian women, they perceived these encounters as primarily social rather than political. For women who were not politically active on the Israeli left prior to the *intifada*,

these meetings were their first opportunity to talk face to face with Palestinian women from the Occupied Territories. Many Israeli-Jewish
women believed that in order to build bridges of trust and understanding between the two communities they must first focus on their shared
experiences as women and establish personal connections. That is to
say, Israeli-Jewish women were not as eager as Palestinian women to
discuss the politics of the Israeli-Palestinian conflict or the Occupation. Instead, they were interested in encounters based on similarities
and grounded in the principle of dialogue between equals.

Despite their differing expectations, which, for the most part, were
not made explicit, both Palestinian and Israeli-Jewish women understood the potential contribution of these encounters to their struggles
and thus were careful not to antagonize their partners. In order to avoid
conflict, issues that could cause controversy were kept off the agenda,
at least during the first two years of the *intifada*. To come to terms with
both the potential and the pitfalls of various encounters and alliances
between Palestinian and Israeli-Jewish women, however, the differences
in these expectations must be examined in relation to the broader
political context that shaped and informed them.

Nearly six and one-half years after the start of the *intifada*, encounters and political alliances between Israeli-Jewish and Palestinian
women are almost nonexistent. This fact is indicative of the crisis in
both the Palestinian and Israeli women's peace movements, which is
directly related to the politics of Middle East peace. As the locus of
political activity and attention shifted from the grassroots level to the
high-visibility diplomacy of the official peace process, women's contribution to and participation in peacemaking has been marginalized. But
the fragile alliances between Israeli-Jewish women and Palestinian
women had already faced serious obstacles even prior to the Madrid
conference and the Declaration of Principles.

The Gulf crisis posed the first major challenge to joint ventures
between women on both sides of the Israeli-Palestinian divide. When
Iraqi missiles were fired at Israel, Israeli women's voices of dissent
against war as a solution to problems were drowned out by the patriotic calls for military action. In addition, the Gulf crisis interrupted
the efforts of Palestinian and Israeli-Jewish women to jointly organize
an international women's peace in Jerusalem. Palestinian women activists involved in the planning of the joint conference still find it hard

to forgive their Israeli counterparts for not contacting them during the six week long curfew and for failing to take a more explicit and unequivocal stand against the Gulf War and against the pro-war positions echoed by large segments of the Israeli peace camp. In the aftermath of the war there were several attempts on both sides of the Israeli-Palestinian divide to reevaluate and strengthen the ties between the Palestinian and Israeli women's movements, these efforts, however, faltered and were often ignored as the Madrid peace process got under way.

From Dialogue to Solidarity and Beyond

The different types of encounters and alliances between Palestinian and Israeli-Jewish women and the dynamics of their relationship are, in many ways, unique to the Israeli-Palestinian context. At the same time, they involve issues and processes that have characterized relationships between women who belong to different cultural, ethnic or national collectivities in other parts of the world. Most accounts of women's alliances in the particular context of the Israeli-Palestinian conflict have focused primarily on various efforts to bring together groups of Palestinian and Israeli-Jewish women, often overlooking differences and conflicts both within and between the groups.

To come to terms with the complex relationship between Palestinian and Israeli-Jewish women, we should not limit our analysis to their commonalities or their occasional collaborative projects. We should also pay close attention to differences and conflicts within and between the groups and in particular to the extent to which they are allowed to surface during the encounters and to the strategies devised to confront them. A careful examination of the relationship between Israeli-Jewish and Palestinian women should begin with a comparison of the different objectives, dynamics, and politics that characterize various types of encounters and alliances.

More particularly, this entails asking questions about aspects such as the demographic composition of groups that have initiated and participated in alliances, about their explicit and implicit objectives and short- and long-term expectations as well as about social and political developments that may strengthen or weaken them. To answer this questions, I suggest we distinguish between three types of encounters: (1) dialogue groups; (2) women's peace conferences; and (3) collaborative projects and solidarity initiatives.

Dialogue Groups

Like the other types of allainces discussed here, dialogue groups are not unique to the relationship between Palestinian and Israeli-Jewish women. The practice of dialogue between adversaries as a means of resolving various conflicts, has existed in different societies throughout history. In recent times, however, dialogue has gained an almost unquestioned status as the preferred means to overcome any conflict. The liberal discourse of dialogue with its emphasis on face-to-face meetings in a neutral environment has shaped many accounts of Middle East politics and, to some extent, became part of everyday common sense.[21] The dialogue format has become particularly common among women's groups in the context of the Israeli-Palestinian conflict since the *intifada* began.

Examination of some of the underlying assumptions of the dialogue format uncovers a number of consistent themes, beginning with a focus on similarities and shared experiences. In the context of the relationship between Israeli-Jewish and Palestinian women the experience of motherhood has been one of the primary commonalities used as a basis for dialogue. A not untypical illustration took place during a dialogue encounter between Israeli and Palestinian women activists in June 1990, in the West Bank town of Jenin. An Israeli-Jewish woman shared both her vision and strategy for the resolution of the Israeli-Palestinian conflict: Palestinian mothers should keep their sons from throwing stones at Israeli soldiers, and Jewish mothers ought to put pressure on their sons not to serve in the Israeli-occupied West Bank and Gaza Strip.[22]

Another example of the centrality of motherhood in women's attempts to address the Israeli-Palestinian conflict is reflected in the fact that Women for Co-Existence proudly took the Hebrew acronym *Neled*, which translates into "we will give birth." The group was established by a few Israeli-Jewish women in the Tel Aviv area following the outbreak of the *intifada* in order to promote dialogue between Jewish and Palestinian women, including Palestinian women who hold

Israeli citizenship. The group visited Palestinian villages and towns both in Israel and in the Occupied Territories, met with Palestinian women activists, and invited them to speak in Israeli-Jewish homes about their experiences and struggles.[23]

It is important to recognize that the recurring emphasis on motherhood in dialogue groups is related to the fact that the focus of dialogue groups tends to be on similarities and shared experiences. Motherhood and the notion of universal sisterhood have been assumed to constitute a common ground for encounters between women on both sides of the Israeli-Palestinian divide. An emphasis on motherhood in the context of dialogue groups, however, is not unique to the Israeli-Palestinian case. Symbols and images associated with motherhood, such as those of life giving and care taking have informed the struggles of women peace activists around the world at least since the turn of the century.[24]

But the relationship between women, motherhood, and peace is not as natural and conflict-free as it is made to seem. Feminist peace activist, Hannah Safran, for example, has voiced uneasiness about the overwhelming use of motherhood as a primary discourse of dialogue between Israeli-Jewish and Palestinian women: "Is our primary role as a women's peace movement to stress that we are mothers and based on the idealization of motherhood argue that we refuse to keep sending our sons to fight? Maybe it is time for us to also stress other identities. To point out that we are not just mothers, that some of us are not mothers (either by choice or not), that we are lesbians and heterosexuals, Ashkenazi and Sepharadic, young and old, wealthy and poor, and that all these diverse identities constitute legitimate locations from which we can voice opposition to war and conquest."[25]

Dialogue groups with their universal presumptions and focus on similarities have not offered a conducive framework for the exploration of questions of identity and difference between or within the groups. Similarly presumed to be universal, but with a slightly different emphasis, the notion of universal sisterhood places a high value on similarities, interpersonal communication, and friendship among individual women. This emphasis has been a widely used framework for women's encounters since early examples of women's support groups and consciousness-raising groups.

The greatest weakness of an emphasis on the commonalities between opposing groups in the dialogue format is that experiences of oppression, structured inequalities, and other differences between the groups are often ignored or downplayed during the encounter because they are seen as impediments to peace and conflict resolution. Nevertheless, since the rationale of dialogue groups appears both reasonable and constructive, those who raise questions about differences in power and privilege among the participants or criticize the liberal assumptions that underlie this mode of encounter, are often portrayed as rejecting the very idea of conflict resolution. As a result, argues Palestinian scholar Mohammed Abu-Nimer, "attempts to establish dialogue and communication between conflicting parties are always welcomed regardless of their content, structure, motivation and outcome. Those who oppose these attempts are usually labeled as 'radicals' or 'fanatics'."[26] Therefore, few women on either side of the Israeli-Palestinian divide have publicly criticized dialogue groups.

The participation of many Israeli-Jewish women in such encounters has been encouraged primarily by liberal positions on both the Israeli-Palestinian conflict and feminism. They believed that through dialogue they could find ways to transcend cultural, historical, and political differences and to unite under the banner of global sisterhood and peace, which could then have a spillover effect onto the Israeli-Palestinian conflict. Palestinian women, on the other hand, carried with them a rather different understanding grounded in their activism as women in the context of a national liberation struggle; their participation in such meetings was motivated first and foremost by pragmatic political reasons. Because their long-term goal was to bring about the end of the occupation, they saw their encounters with Israeli women as an important vehicle for influencing public opinion in Israel in that direction. For them, dialogue was not perceived as a means for overcoming differences and establishing personal relationships with Israeli-Jewish women, but rather a tool of social transformation and political change. These basic differences in objectives and expectations put considerable strains on the liberal dialogue format.

Despite clear attempts by Israeli-Jewish women to unite around commonalities rather than address differences, disparities in power and privilege, as well as other political, cultural, and historical differences separating Israeli-Jewish from Palestinian women surfaced in the dynamics of most encounters. When Palestinian women called attention to the asymmetric nature of the Israeli-Palestinian conflict, and to the fact that women's encounters too mirror the relationship between occupiers and occupied, they were often met with resistance and defensiveness on the part of many Israeli-Jewish women who insisted that a focus on differences and divisions between them might inhibit the goals of dialogue.

Another issue that Israeli-Jewish women tended to overlook was how the format of the meetings further emphasized the disparities in power and privilege between occupiers and occupied because in most cases, Palestinian women from the Occupied Territories were invited to participate in dialogue groups held in the homes of Israeli-Jewish women within Israel. Encounters did not exactly take place in neutral spaces for Palestinian women, who took considerable risks by crossing through the road blocks and checkpoints of the Green Line, not knowing whether their own communities would be under curfew or attack when they returned.

Over time, a number of Palestinian women began to raise critical questions about the dialogue format with its liberal assumptions and presumed symmetry and neutrality, which are often hidden behind the appealing rhetoric of cross-cultural understanding and bridge-building. From their perspective, the dialogue format has been a practice serving primarily the needs of women that belong to the more powerful and privileged group, namely Israeli-Jewish women. Activist Maha Nassar, a leading figure in the Palestinian women's movement, insists that, instead of exposing Palestinian women, particularly those who are very poor and come from refugee camps, to the gap between their living conditions and those of Israeli-Jewish women, "Israeli women ought to come to our communities and see our suffering."[27]

This critique does not rule out encounters with Israeli-Jewish women but rather offers a different format that takes into account the unequal nature of the relations between the two groups. It calls into question the notion of a universal shared experience of women, emphasizing that women are divided not only by nationality but also by class. Rather than accepting that dialogue and liberal bridge-building were inherently helpful, Nassar believes that critical questions must precede adopting these practices. Foremost among such questions is that concerning "what kind of bridges you want to build, between whom and leading to what."[28]

In sum, although women like Nassar tend to agree that the processes of searching for common ground and of learning to respect each other as individuals are important and often result in comforting personal feelings, they insist that in order to build and sustain alliances with Israeli-Jewish women, inequalities in power and privilege rooted in the broader sociopolitical context of the Israeli-Palestinian conflict must be addressed. In other words, experiences of oppression cannot be reconciled simply through interpersonal processes that focus primarily on how women treat each other as individuals in the artificially controlled environment of a women's dialogue group. Some of these concerns, although not all of them, have been addressed in a series of local and international peace conferences designed to explore women's perspectives on the Israeli-Palestinian conflict.

Women's Peace Conferences

Women's peace conferences have extended the basis of encounters between Palestinian and Israeli-Jewish women beyond the shared experiences of women to political positions and joint commitment to the resolution of the Israeli-Palestinian conflict. As a result, encounters involved a focus on both similarities and differences between Palestinian and Israeli-Jewish women.

According to Simone Susskind, President of the Secular Jewish Community of Brussels who organized and sponsored the 1989 international women's peace conference "Israeli women in the peace movement and . . . Palestinian women, who play such an important role in the intifada . . . have dabbled less in politics and are less imprisoned by ideological concepts and less divided by psychological barriers, [and thus] might be more prepared to listen and talk to one another without prejudice."[29] Despite the structure of the conference which treated Jewish and Palestinian women as if they were equal and the fact that it was sponsored by a Jewish woman, Palestinian women saw in the conference an opportunity to share their experiences and political perspectives in order to transform the positions of their Jewish counterparts on the Israeli-Palestinian conflict.

Indeed, the conference in Brussels was a transformative experience for many of its Jewish participants. Rachel Ostrowitz, a member of the Israeli-Jewish delegation, described the conference as "a very important turning point" in her relationship with Palestinian women.[30] The encounter with Palestinian women from the West Bank and Gaza

Strip and from the diaspora, including women who came from Tunis as official representatives of the PLO, triggered new questions and experiences that had a dramatic impact on Ostrowitz's attitudes toward Palestinian women: "the Palestinian women shared difficult experiences of oppression, displacement and violation of basic human rights and needs. Their protest and anger were directed at the state of Israel. Listening to them, I had to ask myself: how shall I, an Israeli citizen, respond and work to change this situation?"[31]

The crucial questions that the Brussels conference triggered for Ostrowitz have been also raised in other local and international conferences and events on the conflict. For example, following the December 1989 women's day for peace, that culminated in a massive march of six thousand women from West to East Jerusalem, the Women and Peace Coalition in Israel which sponsored the day concluded that "the event was successful beyond expectations in terms of level of participation and cooperation between Israeli and Palestinian women. It emphasized the distinguished role that women can play in bringing peace. This success motivated us to seek further and deeper mutual cooperation between Palestinian and Israeli women."[32]

After the conference, the Palestinian women's organizations and Israeli women peace groups were contacted by the Swedish branch of the Women's International League for Peace and Freedom (WILPF) with an initiative to convene an international peace conference in Jerusalem. Consequently, representatives of Palestinian and Israeli women's groups began to meet to jointly plan the December 1990 conference. For a while it seemed that Palestinian and Israeli-Jewish women have built the foundations for a strong alliance. But the Gulf War challenged this perception.

The war and its implications for women's lives and alliances was perceived differently by Palestinian and Israeli-Jewish activists. Israeli women attributed the difficulties they faced in accomplishing their objectives to the Gulf crisis and later to the war. For Palestinian women, on the other, the Gulf War marked a serious disillusionment with their relationship with their Israeli-Jewish counterparts, causing them to rethink the very basis of women's resistance and women's alliances. As a result, Palestinian women began to criticize the very nature and underlying assumptions of women's peace conferences. According to Palestinian scholar and activist Rita Giacaman, many such conferences have been "imposed on Palestinian and Israeli-Jewish women by outsiders who had money from their governments and wanted to have a conference."[33] She argues that there is no need for more conferences, tea parties or dialogue groups and instead calls for "street action that does not necessarily have to be joint."[34] Street action, according to Giacaman, may include demonstrations, collaborative projects, and solidarity initiatives designed to improve the daily lives of people under occupation.

In sum, although peace conferences have moved beyond some of the constraints of dialogue groups and have often taken into account the political context of women's encounters and alliances, they did not challenge the presumed symmetry between Israelis and Palestinians.

Collaborative Projects and Solidarity Initiatives

The transition from women's encounters that focus primarily on dialogue and take place around a conference table to a relationship characterized by collaborative projects and solidarity initiatives requires a strong political commitment. This type of relationship does not focus primarily on similarities and on the shared experiences of women but rather recognizes from the outset the differences, injustices, and inequalities separating Palestinian and Israeli-Jewish women. The ongoing work of the WOFPP is perhaps the best example of this different mode of activism. The creation of alliances between women on both sides of the conflict was never a stated objective for the WOFPP, nevertheless, their work in support of Palestinian women prisoners, which has been coordinated throughout with Palestinian women's organizations in the West Bank and Gaza Strip, has led to the development of strong ties between Israeli-Jewish women and Palestinian women in the Occupied Territories.

The key insight underlying the emphasis on solidarity work is that collaborative and consistent work on a joint project over a significant period of time results in trust and in strong relationships precisely because personal relationships are viewed as a possible, but not necessary, outcome of a political alliance. There is no doubt that persistence is an important measure of credibility for those involved in solidarity work, but it is not enough. Another important measure seems to be the readiness and willingness of Israeli-Jewish women to relinquish the premise of symmetry between Israelis and Palestinians. Unlike dialogue groups and peace conferences, collaborative projects and solidarity initiatives require that Israeli-Jewish women not only acknowledge but also act upon the power and privilege they enjoy both in their interactions with Palestinian women and in the broader sociopolitical context of the Israeli occupation. By confronting these differences, these women have avoided the common trap of coalescing around the most common dimension of their struggle—their gender and shared experience as women—and overlooking crucial differences that are rooted in the political structures and in unequal power relations.

In the context of the Israeli-Palestinian conflict, differences in power relations cannot be overlooked. Recognition of these disparities involve acknowledging that encounters take place not only between Palestinian and Israeli-Jewish women but also between a women's movement informed for the most part by Western feminism and one whose struggle for women's liberation is part of a broader anticolonial liberation struggle, inspired by similar struggles of women in other parts of the world. These differences, however, are not reducible to cultural differences such as those between Western and Middle Eastern women. Rather, they are differences that are political and contextual, stemming from different historical trajectories that dialogue groups and women's peace conferences tend to overlook.

Above all the other dimensions that characterize the encounter between Israeli-Jewish and Palestinian women, the basic one is that an encounter between Palestinian and Israeli-Jewish women is first and foremost an encounter between occupiers and occupied. The disparities in power and privilege between Palestinian and Israeli-Jewish women have their roots in the history of the Israeli-Palestinian conflict in general and in the Israeli occupation of the West Bank and Gaza Strip in particular. They are reflected in the ways cultural differences and multiple interpretations of feminism are articulated and dealt with during the encounters.

Solidarity work is always collaborative, but it must begin with the needs of the disenfranchised group rather than those of the more privileged. In other words, solidarity initiatives carried out by Israeli-Jewish women must be evaluated not only based on the extent of collaboration with Palestinian women but also on the extent to which they focus on the suffering of the occupied rather than on the humanity of the occupier. Even when these two conditions are met, for collaborative projects to succeed, the terms of solidarity need to be constantly negotiated. It should be clear from the outset, however, that the term *negotiation* is not used here to imply that Palestinian and Israeli-Jewish women should have an equal say in determining the nature and scope of a collaborative project. Rather, negotiating the terms of solidarity implies that *before* a solidarity initiative is carried out, Israeli-Jewish women must consult with Palestinian women to determine their needs and priorities and their willingness to collaborate on a particular project.

For many Israeli women peace activists solidarity is not an easy task. According to Israeli-Jewish feminist and peace activist Yvonne Deutsch "many Jewish women, even among those who protest the occupation, have difficulty feeling solidarity with Palestinian women or with the Palestinian people."[35] The problem, she argues, manifests itself not only in the relatively low number of solidarity projects that have been initiated by Israeli-Jewish women since the *intifada* but also in the confusion expressed by some women when Palestinians express solidarity with their efforts to end the occupation. Deutsch describes a particular incident involving some Women in Black in Jerusalem who felt uncomfortable and confused upon "receiving words of support from Palestinian male laborers, who, returning home from a day's work in Israel, would pass them on the road."[36] She concluded that this confusion originates from the apparent contradiction between the encouragement Women in Black receive from Palestinians and the isolation they feel in their own society.[37] Because solidarity work, more than other forms of encounters and alliances, calls into question the distinctions between "us" and "them," the confusion expressed by some Israeli-Jewish women reflects a fear of being perceived as disloyal to their own community.

It would be a mistake, however, to assign all the blame and responsibility to Israeli-Jewish women without the taking into consideration the broader political context, particularly the rigid boundaries of Israeli-Jewish collective identity and the sanctions imposed on those who dare to (or are perceived as trying to) challenge them in any way shape or form. In this context, the engagement of Israeli-Jewish women peace activists with collaborative projects and solidarity work with Palestinian women in the West Bank and Gaza Strip is likely to be perceived as an act of national betrayal by the majority of Israeli society.

The constructed borders between "traitors" and "patriots" and between "us" and "them" have been used as rigid signifiers of collective national identity; those who cross these borders or challenge their rigidity are considered traitors and are forced to pay the price and live "in exile" on the periphery of Israeli-Jewish collectivity. The act of labelling Israeli-Jewish women who engage in solidarity work as traitors has not only legitimized campaigns of fear and intimidation against these women, but has probably kept more women from joining women's peace groups and speaking out against the occupation. At the same time, the more Israeli-Jewish women (and men) are willing to pay the price that often accompanies acts of solidarity, the more difficult it will be for the Israeli authorities to marginalize, discredit and present these human gestures as acts of treason.

Consider, for example, again the work of the WOFPP. These women have utilized the power and privileges that accompany their Israeli citizenship to act as strong advocates on behalf of Palestinian women prisoners. To do this, they had to create for themselves a kind of transformative experience that their original identity—bound by the dominant narrative of Israeli national identity—has forbidden. Creating such a transformative experience is not an easy task. Yet feminist scholar Sandra Harding urges those committed to solidarity projects not to fear the label "traitor" but rather to adopt and use it subversively. For Harding, the affirmation and celebration of "traitorous" identities, is an important act of solidarity with those considered to be "others" or "them."[38]

In the context of the present examination of Palestinian and Israeli-Jewish women's alliances, it implies that to engage in solidarity work, one has to be ready to leave her safe home or step outside the boundaries of the Israeli-Jewish community as it is presently defined, and pay the price that traitors are forced to pay. At the same time, solidarity work is not simply about challenging and relinquishing loyalties; it is grounded in a different set of loyalties and inspired by alternative visions of identity and community.

In conclusion, the Palestinian and the Israeli-Jewish women's movements are in the midst of grappling with and redefining their own identity and direction at this time. Women in both movements have begun to confront crucial questions of identity and difference as well as the complex relationship between dominant interpretations of national identity and other modalities of identity such as gender, ethnicity, religion, class and sexuality, among others. This exploration is likely to provide a common ground for the emergence of contingent, yet stronger, alliances between Palestinian and Israeli-Jewish women. The durability of such alliances will depend to a great extent on the political climate in the Middle East. A drastic improvement in the relationship between Palestinian and Israeli-Jewish women—still primarily a relationship between occupiers and occupied—requires the end of Israeli occupation of the West Bank and Gaza Strip.

Alliances between Israeli-Jewish women and Palestinian women in the West Bank and Gaza Strip are fragile and face constant challenges, originating both from the dynamic and unpredictable political context and from the grave disparities in power and privilege between Israelis and Palestinians—occupiers and occupied. At the same time, it should be recognized that various types of encounters that have taken place between Israeli-Jewish and Palestinian women rest on particular assumptions about gender, the Israeli-Palestinian conflict, and the relationship between them.

The emergence of such alliances depends to a great extent on an unequivocal acknowledgment of power disparities between the two communities and a willingness on the part of Israeli-Jewish women to account for their power and privilege. Future alliances should be built on the basis of recognizing a common yet differing impact of the Israeli-Palestinian conflict on the lives and struggles of Palestinian and Israeli women. Their transformative potential depends on the ability, willingness, and courage of both Israeli-Jewish and Palestinian women to recognize both their shared and different experiences and negotiate the terms of solidarity from this standpoint.

9

Conclusion

➜ "We don't need to wait for a 'feminist Henry Kissinger'," insists Cynthia Enloe, "before we can start articulating a fresh, more realistic approach to international politics. Every time a woman explains how her government is trying to control her fears, her hopes and her labor such a theory is made."[1] One does not have to become an expert on the Israeli-Palestinian conflict, or to master the entire body of literature on gender in international politics, to realize the need to make the role of gender visible in the complex political configurations of the Israeli-Palestinian conflict.

Gender matters. It shapes both directly and indirectly our relationships, daily practices, and understandings of who we are both as individuals and as part of a broader "imagined community." This is a fact that by now should be taken as given. The next time we are asked, in disbelief, to explain once again what exactly has gender to do with particular developments in world politics, we should turn the question around. Let those who continue to think that gender has nothing to do with politics prove their argument. The burden of proof should not be on those who have learned that gender matters, but rather on those who have made gender invisible and who continue to benefit from this invisibility. We should not waste our valuable time, energies, and resources to demonstrate why gender matters but rather move on to examine exactly how it matters in different contexts.

So what do we learn about the Israeli-Palestinian conflict when we recognize that gender matters? First, in addition to the interplay between gender and the politics of the Israeli-Palestinian conflict and

150

the joint and separate struggles of Palestinian women in the West Bank and Gaza Strip and of Israeli-Jewish women, which this book has sought to illuminate, there are numerous other dimensions of the Israeli-Palestinian conflict that are rarely considered in conventional media accounts and academic scholarship. Lost in conventional coverage of the conflict are the gendered dimensions of history, practices, and global arrangements of power that have made the conflict one of the most important forces in shaping the both the individual and collective identities of Palestinians and Israeli-Jews.

Making gender visible is one way to understand how particular ideas about identity and community, informed by certain notions of masculinity, femininity, and gender relations, have become hegemonic at the expense of alternative possibilities. The struggles of Palestinian and Israeli-Jewish women against the occupation of the West Bank and Gaza Strip, and for gender equality within their own societies, suggest new ways of thinking about and working for alternative visions of society where the security of the nation would not render its underprivileged citizens insecure and where the meaning of liberation would extend beyond the national level to include women's liberation as well.

Still, some may argue that the voices, perspectives, and struggles of the Palestinian and Israeli-Jewish women highlighted in this book are not representative of the majority of Jewish women in Israel or Palestinian women in the West Bank and the Gaza Strip. Yet, it is precisely these women's experiences that highlight dimensions of the Israeli-Palestinian conflict that often remain unaddressed. Taking these experiences seriously has a transformative potential in that it makes contestable the often taken-for-granted assumptions behind dominant interpretations of the Israeli-Palestinian conflict, which render gender invisible.

All too often, the widely divergent positions of the people whose lives have been entangled in the conflict are subsumed under the positions of governments or other official representatives, which has the effect of marginalizing voices and perspectives that may be instrumental in the search for and the implementation of conflict resolution initiatives in the Middle East. As a result, alternative visions of what peace might even look like are restricted to the narrow formulations of those presently in power.

In addition to creating space for new interpretations of peace and security, Palestinian and Israeli-Jewish women's struggles for gender equality and for a just resolution of the Israeli-Palestinian conflict challenge the narrow and conventional definition of "women's issues." They demonstrate that all issues, including those of local and international politics, are women's issues and that women's issues are always political. Connections articulated by women activists, such as between gender and the Israeli-Palestinian conflict, address the militarization of people's lives, the spillover of violence from the conflict into women's lives and the links between militarism and sexism. It is by paying attention to these perspectives and voices that the Israeli-Palestinian conflict can be engaged and theorized from a new vantage point.

This vantage point requires that we move beyond simply speaking about women's perspectives on the Israeli-Palestinian conflict and their struggles for a just and lasting peace in the region to include the complementary project of making men visible *as men* and exposing the discourse of militarized masculinity underlying the Israeli-Palestinian conflict and conventional writings about it. In other words, to make gender visible in the context of the Israeli-Palestinian conflict, one must move beyond "the woman question" to include what Kathy Ferguson refers to as "the man question."[2]

The prospects for peace in the Middle East depend upon our ability and courage to call into question the gendered language and assumptions that inform dominant interpretations and practices of the Israeli-Palestinian conflict. Until these frameworks lose some of their power to define how we see and name the Israeli-Palestinian conflict, it will remain difficult for other voices to be heard and taken seriously. As the rich and diverse experiences of Palestinian and Israeli-Jewish women reveal, there are numerous strategies of struggle that can be employed to challenge what Carol Cohn describes as "the dominant voice of militarized masculinity and decontextualized rationality."[3] Over and above all the other objectives I had in mind for this book, I hope that it will contribute both to theoretical and practical discussions about how we can work more effectively to challenge existing structures of power and inequality and at the same time explore new visions of identity and community that are likely to foster a just and lasting peace in the Middle East.

Notes
Bibliography
Index

Notes

1. Introduction

1. Personal conversation, Occupied West Bank, June 1991.

2. Questions of authorship, identity, and representation have inspired a growing body of feminist literature on the politics and practices involved in knowledge production by and about women. See, for example, Chandra T. Mohanty, "Under Western Eyes: Feminist Scholarship and Colonial Discourses," in *Third World Women and the Politics of Feminism*, eds., Chandra T. Mohanty, Ann Russo, and Lourdes Torres (Bloomington: Indiana Univ. Press, 1991), 51–80; Rey Chow, "Violence in the Other Country: China as Crisis, Spectacle, and Woman," in *Third World Women and the Politics of Feminism*, 81–101; Trinh T. Minh-ha, *Woman, Native, Other: Writing Postcoloniality and Feminism* (Bloomington: Indian Univ. Press, 1989); Patti Lather, *Getting Smart: Feminist Research and Pedagogy with/in the Postmodern* (New York: Routledge, 1991); Sherna Berger-Gluck and Daphne Patai, eds., *Women's Words: The Feminist Practice of Oral History,* (New York: Routledge, 1991); and Anne Opie, "Qualitative research, Appropriation of the 'Other' and Empowerment," *Feminist Review* 3 (1991): 52–69. The following texts address the politics of knowledge production in the context of research and writing about women in the Middle East: *Arab Women in the Field: Studying Your Own Society,* ed. Soraya Altorki and Camillia Fawzi El-Solh, (Syracuse: Syracuse Univ. Press, 1988); Marnia Lazreg, "Feminism and Difference: The Perils of Writing as a Woman on Women in Algeria," in eds., *Conflicts in Feminism*, ed. Marianne Hirsch and Evelyn Fox-Keller (New York: Routledge, 1990), 326–48; Rema Hammami and Martina Rieker, "Feminist Orientalism or Orientalist Marxism," *New Left Review* 20 (July–Aug. 1988): 1-7 and Mai Ghossoub, "A Reply to Hammami and Rieker," *New Left Review* (July–Aug. 1988): 8–11. See also Simona Sharoni, "Middle East Politics Through Feminist Lenses: Toward Theorizing International Relations from Women's Struggles," *Alternatives* 18 (1993): 5–28 and Nahla Abdo's critical reading of my article titled, "Middle East Politics Through Feminist Lenses: Negotiating the Terms of Solidarity," *Alternatives* 18 (1993): 29–38.

3. For more detailed accounts of impact of the Israeli occupation on the daily lives of Palestinians in the West Bank and Gaza Strip see Al-Haq (Law in the Service of Man). *Punishing a Nation: Human Rights Violations During the Uprising, December 1987-December 1988* (Boston: South End Press, 1990); Naseer Aruri, ed. *Occupation: Israel Over Palestine.* 2d ed. (Belmont, Mass.: Association of Arab-American University Graduates, 1989); Geiger, H. Jack, Jennifer Leaning, Leon A. Shapiro, and Bennett Simon. *The Casualties of Conflict: Medical Care and Human Rights in the West Bank and Gaza Strip* (Somerville, Mass.: Physicians for Human Rights, 1988); and Middle East Watch. *The Israeli Army and the Intifada: Policies That Contribute to the Killings* (New York: Human Rights Watch, 1990).

2. Feminist Theory, Gender Issues, and Middle East Politics

1. For an overview of women's resistance around the world see V. Spike Peterson and Anne Sisson Runyan, "The Politics of Resistance: Women as Nonstate, Antistate, and Transstate Actors," in *Global Gender Issues* (Boulder, Colo.: Westview Press, 1993), 113-47. There are extensive bodies of literature, documenting the various contexts of women's resistance. Following are some representative references that may serve as starting points for a more extensive exploration of particular struggles. For accounts on women's activism in peace and justice movements see especially Adrienne Harris and Ynestra King, eds., *Rocking the Ship of State: Toward a Feminist Peace Politics* (Boulder, Colo.: Westview Press, 1989) and Harriet Hyman Alonso, *Peace as a Women's Issue: A History of the U.S. Movement for World Peace and Women's Rights* (Syracuse, NY: Syracuse University Press, 1993). For accounts of women's activism on environmental issues see in particular Vandana Shiva, *Staying Alive: Women, Ecology and Development* (London: Zed Books, 1989); Annabel Rodda, *Women and the Environment* (London: Zed Books, 1991) and Irene Diamond and Gloria Feman Orenstein, eds., *Reweaving the World: The Emergence of Ecofeminism* (San Francisco, CA: Sierra Club Books, 1990. For information about women's resistance in the context of national liberation movements see Kumari Jayawardena, *Feminism and Nationalism in the Third World* (London: Zed Books, 1986) and Miranda Davies, ed. *Third World-Second Sex: Women's Struggles and National Liberation* (London: Zed Books, 1983).

2. Chandra T. Mohanty, "Cartographies of Struggles: Third World Women and the Politics of Feminism," in *Third World Women and the Politics of Feminism*, ed. Chandra T. Mohanty, Ann Russo and Lourdes Torres (Bloomington: Indiana Univ. Press 1991), 13.

3. For representative examples, see Perdita Huston, *Third World Women Speak Out* (New York: Praeger, 1979); Cherrie Moraga and Gloria Anzaldua eds., *This Bridge Called My Back: Writings By Radical Women of Color* (New York: Kitchen Table: Women of Color Press, 1983); Barbara Smith, ed., *Home Girls: A Black Feminist Anthology,* (New York: Kitchen Table: Women of Color Press, 1983); Beverley Lindsay, ed., *Comparative Perspectives of Third World Women: The Impact of Race, Sex and Class* (New York: Praeger, 1983); Gloria P. Hull, P. Scott and Barbara Smith, eds., *But Some of Us Are Brave* (New York: Feminist Press, 1982); and Mohanty, "Under Western Eyes."

4. Jane Flax, "Postmodernism and Gender Relations in Feminist Theory," in *Feminism/Postmodernism,* ed. Linda Nicholson (New York: Routledge, 1989), 46.

5. See for example, V. Spike Peterson and Anne Sisson Runyan, *Global Gender Issues* (Boulder, Colo.: Westview Press, 1993); Judith Butler, *Gender Trouble: Feminism and the Subversion of Identity* (New York: Routledge, 1990); and the introduction to Judith Butler and Joan W. Scott, eds. *Feminists Theorize the Political,* (New York: Routledge, 1992).

6. Ibid.

7. Judith Butler, *Gender Trouble,* 3.

8. Dr. Ashrawi was not present in the official face-to-face negotiations that began in Madrid because she is a resident of East Jerusalem and former Israeli Prime Minister Yitzhak Shamir vetoed the participation of Palestinians from East Jerusalem in the negotiations in order to keep the future of Jerusalem off the agenda.

9. For detailed accounts of the struggles of Palestinian women in the West Bank and Gaza Strip since the outbreak of the *intifada,* see, for example, Phillipa Strum, *The Women Are Marching: The Second Sex and the Palestinian Revolution* (New York: Lawrence Hill Books, 1992); Joost Hiltermann, *Behind the Intifada: Labor and Women's Movements in the Occupied Territories* (Princeton: Princeton Univ. Press, 1991); Nahla Abdo, "Women of the *intifada:* Gender, Class and National Liberation," *Race & Class* 32, no. 4 (1991): 19–34; Suha Sabbagh, "Palestinian Women Writers and the *Intifada,*" *Social Text* 22 (Spring 1989): 1–19; and Samira Haj, "Palestinian Women and Patriarchal Relations," *Signs: Journal of Women in Culture and Society,* 17, no. 4, (Summer 1992): 761–78.

10. Cynthia H. Enloe, *Bananas, Beaches and Bases: Making Feminist Sense of International Politics (Berkeley: Univ. of California Press, 1989),* 13.

11. Ibid.

12. Stephen Engelberg, "For the Unlikely Middleman From Norway, Public Thanks," *New York Times,* 14 Sept., 1993, A4; Alon Pinkas, "Jerusalem–Oslo–Tunis: The Crystallization of the Accord," *Ma'ariv,* 3 Sept. 1993, pp. 4–5 (Hebrew); Nachum Barnea and Shimon Shifer, "The Norwegian Connection," *Yediot Achronot,* 2–3 (Hebrew).

13. Ibid.

14. See *Yediot Achronot,* 10 Sept. 1993, 22 (Hebrew).

15. Enloe, *Bananas, Beaches and Bases,* 1–18.

16. See Ann Tickner, *Gender in International Relations: Feminist Perspectives on Achieving Global Security* (New York: Columbia Univ. Press, 1992), 1–25.

17. Wendy Brown, *Manhood and Politics* (Totowa, N. J.: Rowman and Littlefield, 1988), 4.

18. Enloe, *Bananas, Beaches and Bases,* 11.

19. An excerpt from Rabin's speech as reprinted in *New York Times,* 14 Sept., 1993, A12.

20. Carol Cohn, "Sex and Death in the Rational World of Defense Intellectuals," in *Peace: Meanings, Politics, Strategies,* ed. Linda Rennie Forcey (New York: Praeger, 1989), 64.

21. Cynthia Enloe, "Womanandchildren: Making Feminist Sense of the Persian Gulf Crisis," *Village Voice,* 25 Sept. 1990, 29.

22. *New York Times,* 14 Sept. 1993, A12.

23. My use of the term "gender-sensitive lens" draws primarily on Peterson's and Runyan's discussion of gender as a lens for interpreting world politics in *Global Gender Issues.*

24. For a broader theoretical discussion of the relevance of the metaphor of gender-sensitive lenses for research and feminist interventions, see Donna Haraway, "Situated Knowledges: The Science Question in Feminism and the Privilege of Partial Perspective," *Feminist Studies* 14, no. 3 (1988): 575–99; Christine Sylvester, "The Emperors' Theories and Transformations: Looking at the Field Through Feminist Lenses," in *Transformations in Global Political Economy,* ed. Dennis Piragas and Christine Sylvester (London: Macmillan, 1990), 230–53; and Peterson and Runyan, 1–44.

25. *New York Times,* 14 Sept. 1993, A12.

26. Ibid.

27. For further discussion of this point, see Nira Yuval-Davis, "The Jewish Collectivity," in *Women in the Middle East,* ed. The Khamsin Collective (London: Zed Books, 1987); Nira Yuval-Davis and Floya Anthias, eds., *Woman-Nation-State* (London: Macmillan, 1989); and Simona Sharoni, "Homefront as Battlefield: Gender, Military Occupation and Violence Against Women," in *Women and the Israeli Occupation: The Politics of Change,* ed. Tamar Mayer (New York: Routledge, 1994).

28. The phrase "theorizing from women's struggles" is a synthesis of Mohanty's exploration of "cartographies of struggle" and Harding's emphasis on "thinking from women's lives." See Mohanty, "Cartographies of Struggle" and Sandra Harding, *Whose Science? Whose Knowledge? Thinking from Women's Lives* (New York: Cornell Univ. Press, 1991).

29. Mohanty, "Cartographies of Struggle," 39.

30. For example, see Minnie Bruce Pratt, "Identity: Skin, Blood, Heart," in *Yours in Struggle: Three Feminist Perspectives on Anti-Semitism and Racism,* by Elly Bulkin, Minnie Bruce Pratt, and Barbara Smith (New York: Firebrand Books,1984), 9–63; Gloria Anzaldua, *Borderlands/La Frontera: The New Mestiza* (San Francisco: Aunt Lute Books, 1987); Haraway; Chandra T. Mohanty and Biddy Martin "Feminist Politics: What's Home Got to Do with It?" in *Feminist Studies/Critical Studies.* ed. Teresa de Lauretis (Bloomington: Indiana Univ. Press, 1986), 191–212 and Chandra T. Mohanty, "Feminist Encounters: Locating the Politics of Experience," in *Destabilizing Theory: Contemporary Feminist Debates,* ed. Michele Barrett and Anne Phillips, (Stanford,: Stanford Univ. Press, 1992) 74–92.

31. See for example, Elizabeth Fernea and Basima Bezirgan, eds. *Middle East Muslim Women Speak* (Austin: Univ. of Texas Press, 1977); Lois Beck and Nikki Keddie, eds. *Women in the Muslim World* (Cambridge, Mass.: Harvard Univ. Press, 1978); Judith Tucker, *Women in Nineteenth Century Egypt* (New York: Cambridge Univ. Press, 1985); Margot Badran and Miriam Cooke, eds. *Opening the Gates: A Century of Arab Feminist Writing* (Bloomington: Indiana Univ. Press, 1990); and Nikki R. Keddie and Beth Baron, eds. *Women in Middle Eastern History: Shifting Boundaries in Sex and Gender* (New Haven: Yale Univ. Press, 1991).

32. For more detailed discussions on the history of women's struggles in the Arab world, see Leila Ahmed, "Feminism and Feminist Movements in the Middle East, in *Women and Islam,* ed. Aziz al-Hibri (New York: Pergamon, 1982), 153–168; Badran,

"Dual Liberation," and "Independent Women: More Than a Century of Feminism in Egypt," in *Arab Women: Old Boundaries, New Frontiers*, ed. Judith Tucker (Bloomington: Indiana Univ. Press, 1993), 195–207; and Mervat Hatem, "Toward the Development of Post-Islamist and Post-Nationalist Feminist Discourses in the Middle East," in *Arab Women: Old Boundaries, New Frontiers*, ed. Judith Tucker (Bloomington: Indiana Univ. Press, 1993), 29–48.

33. Orayb Aref Najjar with Kitty Warnock, *Portraits of Palestinian Women* (Salt Lake City: Univ. of Utah Press, 1992), xii.

34. Ibid, x.

35. Arlene Elowe MacLeod, *Accommodating Protest: Working Women, the New Veiling, and Change in Cairo* (New York: Columbia Univ. Press, 1991); and Arlene Elowe MacLeod, "Hegemonic Relations and Gender Resistance: The New Veiling as Accommodating Protest in Cairo," *Signs*, (Spring 1992): 533–557.

36. MacLeod, "Hegemonic Relations," 537.

37. For another example of a complex, detailed and contextualized account of the practice of veiling in Palestinian society in the West Bank and Gaza Strip during the *intifada*, see Rema Hammami, "Women, the Hijab, and the *Intifada*," *Middle East Report* 164/165: 24–31.

38. Youssef M. Ibrahim, "Fundamentalists Impose Culture on Egypt," The *New York Times*, Thursday, 3 Feb. 1994, sec. A.

39. Ibid, A10.

40. Orientalism refers to the view according to which the Orient is antithetical to and radically different from the West. For an in-depth examination of the social and political implications of orientalism, see Edward W. Said, *Orientalism* (New York: Vintage, 1979). For more on the representation of Middle Eastern women see, for example, Zjaleh Hajibashi, "Feminism or Ventriloquism: Western Presentations of Middle Eastern Women," *Middle East Report* 172, (Sep./Oct. 1991): 43–45. See also Judy Mabro, *Veiled Half Truths: Western Travellers' Perceptions of Middle Eastern Women* (New York: St. Martin's Press, 1991).

41. See Nayereh Tohidi, "Gender and Islamic Fundamentalism: Feminist Politics in Iran, in *Third World Women and the Politics of Feminism*, ed. Chandra T. Mohanty, Ann Russo, and Lourdes Torres (Bloomington: Indiana Univ. Press, 1991), 51–80 and Afsaneh Najmabadi, "Hazards of Modernity and Morality: Women, State and Ideology in Contemporary Iran," in *Women, Islam and the State*, ed. Deniz Kandiyoti (Philadelphia: Temple Univ. Press, 1991), 48–76.

42. *The Village Voice*, 25 Sept. 1990, p. 30.

43. Deniz Kandiyoti, "Strategies for Feminist Scholarship in the Middle East," Paper presented at the 27th Annual Meeting of the Middle East Studies Association (MESA), Nov. 1993, 1.

44. See for example, Suha Sabbagh and Ghada Talhami, eds. *Images and Reality: Palestinian Women under Occupation and in the Diaspora* (Washington, D.C.: Institute for Arab Women's Studies, 1990); Nahid Toubia, ed. *Women of the Arab World: The Coming Challenge* (London: Zed Books, 1988); Haleh Afshar, ed. *Women in the East: Peceptions, Realities, and Struggles for Liberation* (New York: St. Martin's Press, 1992); and Najjar with Warnock, *Portraits of Palestinian Women*.

45. Margot Badran and Miriam Cooke, *Opening the Gates: A Century of Arab Feminist Writing,* (Bloomington: Indiana Univ. Press, 1990), xv–xvi.

46. Ibid, xix.

47. See in particular Keddi's and Baron's edited anthology, *Women in Middle Eastern History,* and Tucker, *Women in Nineteenth Century Egypt.*

48. See for example, Deniz Kandiyoti, *Women, Islam, and the State* (Philadelphia: Temple Univ. Press, 1992); Valentine M. Moghadam, *Modernizing Women: Gender and Social Change in the Middle East* (Boulder, Colo: Lynne Rienner, 1993); and *Gender and National Identity: Women and Politics in Muslim Societies* (London: Zed Books, 1994).

49. See for example, Julie Peteet, *Gender in Crisis: Women and the Palestinian Resistance Movement.* (New York: Columbia Univ. Press, 1991) and MacLeod, *Accommodating Protest,* and Leila Ahmed, *Women and Gender in Islam: Historical Roots of a Modern Debate* (New Haven and London: Yale Univ. Press, 1992).

3. Nationalisms, Gender, and the Israeli-Palestinian Conflict

1. For a broader theoretical discussion about imagined communities and the processes and practices involved in their consolidation, see Benedict Anderson, *Imagined Communities: Reflections on the Origins and Spread of Nationalism* (London: Verso, 1983). For a gendered analysis of the consolidation of nations as imagined communities, see Yuval-Davis, *Woman-Nation-State;* and Andrew Parker, Mary Russo, Doris Sommer, and Patricia Yaeger, eds., *Nationalisms & Sexualities,* (New York: Routledge, 1992). For an anlaysis of the impact of the relationship between gender and the politics of the Israeli-Palestinian conflict on the construction of an Israeli-Jewish "imagined community," see Yuval-Davis, "The Jewish Collectivity."

2. Deniz Kandiyoti, "Identity and Its Discontents: Women and the Nation," *Millennium: Journal of International Studies* 20, no. 3 (1991), 431.

3. Enloe, *The Morning After,* 232–33.

4. Enloe, *Bananas, Beaches, and Bases;* 61.

5. Quoted in Lesely Hazleton, *Israeli Women: The Reality Behind the Myths* (New York: Simon and Schuster, 1977), 63.

6. See Yuval-Davis, "The Jewish Collectivity."

7. Ibid., 82–84.

8. Abdo, "Women of the *Intifada,*" 25.

9. For more on the distinction between the two forms of nationalism discussed here, see Abdo, "Women of the *Intifada,*" 22–26.

10. See "Introduction" in Parker et al.

11. Abdo, "Women of the *Intifada,*" 30.

12. *Um al-Asirah* means "the mother of a woman prisoner." In most Arab societies it is customary to honor people by referring to them as the parents of their eldest son. For example if the name of the eldest son is Ibrahim, his mother is known in the community as *Um Ibrahim* and his father as *Abu Ibrahim.* The linguistic construct *Um al-Asirah* is used proudly by a mother of a daughter, emphasizing the active political participation of Palestinian women during the *intifada.*

13. Abdo, "Women of the *Intifada*," 30.

14. Ibid.

15. This argument is based on a similar contention by Winifred Woodhull who argued that "women embody Algeria not only for Algerians . . . but also for the French colonizers." See Winifred Woodhull, "Unveiling Algeria," *Genders*, 10 (Spring 1991), 17.

16. Ibid.

17. Marcia Freedman, *Exile in the Promised Land: A Memoir* (New York: Firebrand Books, 1990), 108.

18. See for example David Campbell, *Writing Security: United States Foreign Policy and the Politics of Identity* (Minneapolis: Univ. of Minnesota Press, 1992).

19. For a critical though ungendered examination of the central role the Holocaust played in the construction of Israeli-Jewish collective identity, see Tom Segev, *The Seventh Million: The Israelis and the Holocaust* (Jerusalem: Maxwell-Macmillan-Keter, 1991) (Hebrew).

20. Enloe, *The Morning After*, 250.

21. Ibid., 247–28.

22. Guela Cohen cited in Lesley Hazleton, 63.

23. Nira Yuval-Davis, *Israeli Women and Men: Divisions Behind the Unity* (London: Change, 1982). See also Anne Bloom, "Women in the Defense Forces," in *Calling the Equality Bluff: Women in Israel*, ed. Barbara Swirski and Marilyn Safir (New York: Pergamon Press, 1991), 128–38.

24. Freedman; Hazelton; and Yuval-Davis, *Israeli Women and Men*.

25. Ibid.

26. Yuval-Davis, *Israeli Women and Men*, 16.

27. These numbers were cited in 1988 by Amira Dotan, Israel's first woman general. See interview with Dotan in Swirski and Safir, *Calling the Equality Bluff*, 139–41.

28. Mary Layoun, "Telling Spaces: Palestinian Women and the Engendering of National Narratives," in *Nationalisms & Sexualities*, ed. Andrew Parker, Mary Russo, Doris Sommer, and Patricia Yeager (New York: Routledge, 1992), 411.

29. See the official translation of the Palestinian Declaration of Independence in *Journal of Palestine Studies* 70 (Winter 1989), 213–23.

30. Kandiyoti, "Identity and Its Discontents," 432.

31. Eileen Kuttab, "The *Intifada* and some Women's Social Issues," in a report from the conference held under the same title in December 1990 in Jerusalem and published by the Women's Studies Committee at the Bisan Center. (Ramallah: Bisan Center, 1991), 8.

32. Ibid., 10.

33. Rita Giacaman, "An Uneasy Peace in the Middle East for a Palestinian." *Ms.* (Jan.–Feb. 1994) 10.

34. See, for example, Kathy Glavanis, "The Women's Movement, Feminism, and the National Struggle in Palestine: Unresolved Contradictions," *Journal of Gender Studies*, 1, no. 4 (Nov. 1992): 468; and Philippa Strum, *The Women Are Marching*, 162.

35. This conversation took place in the course of an encounter between Palestinian women activists and Israeli-Jewish and American women in the West Bank town of Jenin, in June 1990.

36. See in particular Robin Morgan, ed., *Sisterhood is Powerful: An Anthology of Writings from the Women's Liberation Movement* (New York: Vintage, 1970).

37. Bell hooks, *Talking Back: Thinking Feminist, Thinking Black* (Boston: South End Press, 1989), 106.

38. Jenny Bourne, "Homelands of the Mind: Jewish Feminism and Identity Politics," *Race & Class*, 19(1987): 2.

39. See, for example, Rosmary Ridd and Helen Callaway, eds., *Women and Political Conflict: Portraits of Struggle in Times of Crisis*, (New York: New York Univ. Press, 1987).

40. See interview with Radwa Basiir in Najjar, 87–95.

41. Najjar, 88.

42. Interview, Haifa, Israel May 1990, in Sharoni, "Conflict Resolution," 211–12.

43. Ibid., 212.

44. Ibid.

4. Palestinian Women's Resistance: History, Context, and Strategies

1. See, for example, Philippa Strum, *The Women Are Marching: The Second Sex and the Palestinan Revolution* (New York: Lawrence Hill Books, 1992); Joost Hiltermann, *Behind the Intifada: Labor and Women's Movements in the Occupied Territories* (Princeton: Princeton Univ. Press, 1991); Kitty Warnock, *Land Before Honour: Palestinian Women in the Occupied Territories* (New York: Monthly Review Press and Basington: Macmillan, 1990); Nahla Abdo, "Women of the *Intifada*: Gender, Class, and National Liberation," *Race & Class* 32, no. 4 (1991): 19–34; Suha Sabbagh, "Palestinian Women Writers and the *Intifada*," *Social Text* 22 (Spring 1989): 1–19; Samira Haj, "Palestinian Women and Patriarchal Relations," *Signs: Journal of Women in Culture and Society* 17, no. 4: 761–78; and Souad Dajani, "Palestinian Women under Israeli Occupation: Implications for Development," in *Arab Women: Old Boundaries, New Frontiers*, ed. Judith Tucker (Bloomington: Indiana Univ. Press, 1993), 149–53.

2. This tendency is more pronounced in literature aimed toward audiences in North America and in Europe who were not familiar with the historical development of the Palestinian women's movement and thus were both surprised and intrigued by the volume of women's political participation.

3. For a broader discussion of the relative neglect of women's history in the Middle East, see Nikki R. Keddie, "Introduction: Deciphering Middle Eastern Women's History," in *Women in Middle Eastern History: Shifting Boundaries in Sex and Gender*, ed. by Nikki R. Keddie and Beth Baron (New Haven: Yale Univ. Press, 1991), 1–22.

4. Ibid., 1.

5. Ibid.

6. For more on the stereotypical depictions of women in the Middle East and their political implications see Sharoni, "Middle East Politics Through Feminist Lenses," 11–6.

7. See, for example, Rosemary Sayigh, *Palestinians: From Peasants to Revolutionaries* (London: Zed, 1979); Strum, *The Women Are Marching*; Hiltermann, *Behind*

the *Intifada*; Peteet, *Gender in Conflict:* Sabbagh and Talhami, eds., *Images and Reality*; and Judith Tucker, "Ties That Bound: Women and Family in Eighteenth- and Nineteenth-Century Nablus," in *Women in Middle Eastern History*, ed. Keddie and Baron, 233–53.

8. Rosemary Sayigh, "Encounters with Palestinian Women under Occupation," *Journal of Palestine Studies* 40, no. 4 (Summer 1981): 3.

9. Ibid.

10. This particular account of Palestinian women's activism during the period of 1917–1948 draws upon the historical overview provided in Mateil Mogannam's, *The Arab Woman and the Palestine Problem* (London: Herbert Joseph, 1937. Reprinted, Westport, Conn.: Hyperion Press, 1976).

11. See Noha S. Ismail, "The Palestinian Women's Struggle for Independence: A Historical Perspective," in *The Third Wave: Feminist Perspectives on Racism*, ed. Jacqui Alexander, Lisa Albrecht, Sharon Day, Mab Segrest, and Norma Alarcon (New York: Kitchen Table: Woman of Color Press, 1993). For more on the rise of Palestinian nationalism, see Muhammad Y. Muslin, The Origins of Palestinian Nationalism (New York: Columbia Univ. Press, 1988).

12. Ibid. Rosemary Sayigh stresses that the 1921 establishment of the Palestinian Women's Union was significant in that it was the first political, cross-sectarian women's union. She points out, however, that women's social associations, mainly sectarian, were active in Palestine since the late Ottoman times. See Rosemary Sayigh, "Palestinian Women: A Case of Neglect," in *Portraits of Palestinian Women*, ed. Orayab Najjar with Kitty Warnock, (Salt Lake City: Univ. of Utah Press, 1992), 4.

13. Ibid. See also Antonius, 26–27; Rosemary Sayigh, "Palestinian Women," 4–5; and Joost Hiltermann 128–29.

14. Ibid.

15. Sayigh, "Palestinian Women," 5.

16. Ibid., 4–5; Hiltermann, 129; and Ismail, 3.

17. Ibid.

18. Ibid. See also Ted Swedenburg, "Palestinian Women in the 1936–1939 Revolt: Implications for the Intifada." Paper presented at the Marxism Now: Tradition and Difference Conference, Univ. of Massachusetts, Amherst, Dec. 2, 1989; and Elise Young, *Keepers of the History: Women and the Israeli-Palestinian Conflict* (New York: Pergamon Press, 1992), 141–48.

19. Hiltermann, 129.

20. Sayigh, "Palestinian Women," 5.

21. See Ismail, 4; Hiltermann, 129; and Sayigh, "Palestinian Women," 5–6. For a detailed overview of this period which unfortunately does not deal specifically with its implications for women's lives and struggles, see Warnock, 6–10.

22. Sayigh, "Palestinian Women," 5.

23. Ibid.

24. Ibid. 5–6.

25. According to Joost Hiltermann, few Palestinian women's groups were explicitly involved in national or women's issues because "the Jordanian regime effectively prevented political organizing by means of harsh repression (banning of political

parties, imprisonment of leaders, expulsions to the East Bank), and sought to control existing institutions by bureaucratic means (for example, through funding), thus defining the conservative character of most organizations." Hiltermann, 129.

26. Laila Jammal, *Contributions by Palestinian Women to the National Struggle for Liberation* (Washington, D.C.: Middle East Public Relations, 1985), 23.

27. Sayigh, "Palestinian Women," 6. Sayigh points out that "with the beginning of *feda'yyiin* (armed struggle) operations in the early sixties, some women became supporters of the still-clandestine resistance organizations." Yet, she notes that "open recruitment of women only began after the Battle of Karameh in 1968" (p. 7). For a personal account of a well-known Palestinian woman who played an active role in the armed struggle during that time, see Leila Khaled, *My People Shall Live: The Autobiography of a Revolutionary* (London: Hodder and Stoughton, 1973).

28. Ibid, 6–7.

29. Jammal, 32.

30. Hiltermann, 129–30.

31. Usama Khalid, "A Palestinian History of Woman's Struggle," *Al-Fajr Jerusalem Palestinian Weekly*, 8 March 1985.

32. Jammal, 32.

33. Hiltermann, 130; Sayigh, "Palestinian Women," 7.

34. Ghada Talhami, "Women Under Occupation: The Great Transformation," in *Images and Reality: Palestinian Women under Occupation and in the Diaspora*, ed. Suha Sabbagh and Ghada Talhami (Washington, D.C.: Institute of Arab Women's Studies, 1990), 15-27.

35. Ibid. See also Susan Rockwell, "Palestinian Women Workers in the Israeli-Occupied Gaza Strip." *Journal of Palestine Studies* 14, no. 2 (Winter 1985); Nahla Abdo-Zu'bi, *Family, Women and Social Change in the Middle East: The Palestinian Case* (Toronto: Scholars Press, 1987); and Suha Hindiye and Afaf Ghazawneh, "The Socio-economic Conditions of Female Wage Labour in the West Bank," in *Palestinian Women: Identity and Experience*, ed. Ebba Augustin, (London: Zed Books, 1993), 68–75.

36. Islah Jad, "From Salons to the Popular Committees: Palestinian Women, 1919–1989" in *Intifada: Palestine at the Crossroads*, ed. Jamal R. Nassar and Roger Heacock, (New York: Bırzeit Unıv. and Praeger, 1990), 129.

37. See Sayigh, "Palestinian Women," 7, and Jad. According to Jad, "in the early days of the occupation, Israel ignored women, since only a handful were actually imprisoned. However, by 1968, women prisoners totalled one hundred, mainly accused of contacting fedayeen, concealing weapons, incitement, or membership in armed organizations." (p. 129).

38. Sayigh, "Palestinian Women," 7.

39. Jad, 129.

40. Ibid., 130. See also Hiltermann, 130–31; and Warnock, 162–64.

41. Rita Giacaman, "Reflections on the Palestinian Women's Movement in the Israeli Occupied Territories," Unpublished Manuscript, Birzeit Univ., West Bank, May 1987. Quoted in Hiltermann, 130.

42. Ibid.

43. See Jad, 130.

44. Ibid. See also Hiltermann, 131.

45. See, for example, Strum, 59; Ismail, 6–7; and Hilterman, 131.

46. See Strum, 59–78; Jad, 131–32; Hiltermann, 131–54; Warnock, 164–75; and Sayigh, "Palestinian Women," 9–10.

47. Siham Barghouti quoted in Warnock, 165.

48. According to Rosemary Sayigh, these surveys represented the first attempt by any Palestinian women's group to examine the living conditions and needs of women in the West Bank. See Sayigh, "Encounters with Palestinian Women," 18.

49. Strum, *The Women are Marching*, 62.

50. Ibid.

51. Hiltermann, *Behind the Intifada*, 132.

52. Rita Giacaman in Philippa Strum, *The Women Are Marching*, 63.

53. Ibid.

54. For a detailed overview of the structure of the PLO and its different factions see Helena Cobban, *The Palestinian Liberation Organization: People, Power, and Politics*, (Cambridge: Cambridge Univ. Press, 1984), 139–67.

55. Hiltermann, *Behind the Intifada*, 133–36; Strum, *The Women Are Marching*, 63–64.

56. Ibid.

57. Hiltermann, 134–36.

58. Ibid.

59. See Souad Dajani, "Palestinian Women Under Israeli Occupation: Implications for Development," in *Arab Women: Old Boundaries, New Frontiers*, (Bloomington: Indiana Univ. Press, 1993), 119–20 and Hiltermann, *Behind the Intifada*, 149–53.

5. Palestinian Women and the *Intifada*

1. Jad, "From Salons to the Popular Committees," and Hiltermann.

2. Ibid.

3. Jad, 133.

4. The report was issued by the Federation of Palestinian Women's Action Committees in March 1988, and is cited in Hiltermann, 194.

5. See Rema Hammami, "The Role of the Woman on the levels of Politics and Struggle in the *Intifada*: A Critical Approach" (paper presented at "The Intifada and Some Women's Social Issues" Conference, Women's Studies Committee/Bisan Center, Ramallah, Occupied West Bank, Dec. 1990).

6. See especially the edited anthology by Ridd and Callaway. It includes a chapter on Palestinian women's resistance, written by Rosemary Sayigh and Julie Peteet, "Between Two Fires: Palestinian Women in Lebanon," 106–37. See also Peteet, especially 128–34.

7. Jad, 133.

8. Ibid.

9. Ibid, 133–34.

10. Hiltermann, 194.

11. Hammami, "The Role of the Woman," 16.

12. Jad, 135.

13. Ibid.

14. Kuttab, conference report 10.

15. Lisa Taraki, "Women's Organizations in Palestine," in *Directory of Palestinian Women's Organizations*, The Women's Studies Committee/Bisan Research and Development Center (Ramallah: Hussary Press, 1993), xiv.

16. The newly founded centers that focus primarily on providing services and advice to women on particular topics include the Center for Legal Aid and Counseling in Jerusalem, which provides Palestinian women with free legal advice, educates women about their status under the law, and offers counseling services. Another is the Family Development Center, which aims to promote family development through courses on women's health and sex education. For more information see the *Directory of Palestinian Women's Organizations*.

17. Ibid., 57.

18. For a more elaborate discussion on feminist action research, see Sharoni, "Conflict Resolution," 20–35. See also the introduction to this book.

19. *Directory of Palestinian Women's Organizations*, 57.

20. The mission statement of the Women's Studies Center appears on the back of its bimonthly English-language publication *Sparks*.

21. This information is based primarily on *Sparks*, and on my conversation with Dr. Suha Hindieh, the center's director in August 1993.

22. Bisan, *Directory*, 83.

23. Ibid.

24. Ibid.

25. *Sparks*, December 1991.

26. The Conference's report in English and in Arabic can be obtained from the Women's Studies Committee at Bisan, P.O Box 725, YMCA Building, 2d Floor, Ramallah City via Israel.

27. For an excellent article on the campaign to impose the *hijab* in Gaza, see Hammami, "Women, the Hijab and the Intifada," 24–28.

28. My interpretation draws on several conversations with Eileen Kuttab, the coordinator of the Women's Studies Committee at Bisan and the chair of the conference's planning committee, May–Aug. 1991, in East Jerusalem. According to other sources, the decision not to focus solely on the hijab reflected the center's fear of calling a major conference on an issue that might alienate too many people. See Strum, 221.

29. Men who spoke at the conference were Mr. Izzat Abdul Hadi, Director of the Bisan Center, Mr. Faisal Husseini, Director of the Arab Studies Society and, at the time, the number one Fatah person in the Occupied Territories, and Dr. Riad Al-Malki from Birzeit University.

30. "The Intifada and Some Women's Social Issues," conference report 11. For more on the move toward "home economy" during the *intifada* and on women's contributions to this particular project, especially through the establishment of women's cooperatives, see Jad, 135–36 and Strum, 74–78, 135–36, 207–08.

31. For more detailed analyses on the impact of the Gulf crisis and war on Palestinian society in the West Bank and Gaza Strip, see Hanan Mikhail Ashrawi, "The Other Occupation: The Palestinian Response"; and Samir Halaileh, "The Gulf Crisis and the Economy in the Occupied Territories," in *Beyond The Storm: A Gulf Crisis Reader,* ed. Phyllis Bennis and Michel Moushabeck (New York: Olive Branch Press, 1991).

32. See Steve Niva, "The Battle is Joined," in *Beyond The Storm: A Gulf Crisis Reader,* ed. Phyliss Bennis and Michael Moushebeck (New York: Olive Branch Press, 1991), 61–62.

33. Strum, 245–47.

34. See Penny Rosenwasser, *Voices from a "Promised Land": Palestinian and Israeli Peace Activists Speak Their Hearts,* (Willimantic, Conn.: Curbstone Press, 1992), 187–99.

35. Initially Palestinians in the West Bank and Gaza Strip were not given gas masks. But when the Israeli government began to distribute masks to Jewish settlers in the Occupied Territories, a Palestinian sued in the Israeli Supreme Court for equal treatment under the Geneva convention. The government argued that Palestinians did not need gas masks since the Occupied Territories were an unlikely target. Nevertheless, the court ordered the Israeli administration to distribute gas masks to Palestinians. At that point, the administration claimed that it did not have enough masks. According to several accounts, military officials admitted privately that they were afraid if Palestinians had gas masks, they might use them to protect themselves against Israeli tear gas once the war was over.

36. This information is based primarily on my conversations with Palestinian women activists during the summer of 1990. The split in the DFLP occurred between a faction led by Yassir Abdel-Rabbo, which backs a two-state solution, and DFLP head Nayef Hawatmeh and his supporters, who insist that the current endorsement of a two-state solution is premature and that the solution to the Israeli-Palestinian conflict should be determined in the course of an international peace conference.

37. Strum, 253.

38. See the conference report, "Women's Studies Center Holds Conference on Domestic Violence Against Women," *Sparks* (Dec. 1991): 2–3.

39. Ibid., 3.

40. Ibid., 2.

41. *Voice of Women,* 7 Feb. 1992.

42. Ibid, 4.

43. Quoted in Rita Giacaman and Penny Johnson, "Searching for Strategies: The Palestinian Women's Movement in the New Era," *Middle East Report* 186 (Jan.–Feb. 1994), 24.

44. Ibid.

45. Ibid., 25.

46. For detailed accounts of the deportations, see the Jan. and Feb. 1993 issues of *News From Within,* an independent political newsletter published by the Alternative Information Center, P.O. Box 31417, Jerusalem. For more information on the closure, see the May–June 1993 issue of *Challenge,* a magazine of the Israeli left, P.O. Box 32107, Jerusalem 91320.

47. See JMCC Weekly Report, 11–17 July 1993, Jerusalem Media & Communication Center, P.O. Box 25047, East Jerusalem.

48. For more information on the Gaza and Jericho First plan and on the September 1993 Declaration of Principles, see *Challenge* 21 (Sep.–Oct. 1993) and Middle East Report 186 (Jan.–Feb. 1994).

49. See "Women of the Opposition Unite," Maya Rosenfeld's interview with Maha Nassar and Aida Issawi, *Challenge*, 22 (Nov.–Dec. 1993), 9.

50. Ibid.

51. This interpretation is based on conversations with Palestinian women activists, Ramallah, November 1993.

6. Israeli-Jewish Women's Struggles: History, Context, and Strategies

1. See, for example, Hazleton; Yuval-Davis, *Israeli Women and Men*; Swirski and Safir, *Calling the Equality Bluff*; Simona Sharoni, "Is Feminism a Threat to National Security?" *Ms.* 3, no. 4 (Jan./Feb. 1993): 18–22; and Yael Azmon and Dafna N. Izraeli, eds., *Women in Israel*, (New Brunswick, N.J.: Transaction Publishers, 1993).

2. Dafna Izraeli, "The Women's Workers' Movement: First Wave Feminism in Pre-State Israel," in *Pioneers and Homemakers: Jewish Women in Pre-State Israel*, ed. Deborah Bernstein (Albany: State Univ. of New York Press, 1992), 184.

3. Deborah Bernstein, "In Search of a New Female Identity: Pioneering Women in Prestate Israeli Society," *Shofar: An Interdisciplinary Journal of Jewish Studies* 9, no. 4 (Summer 1991): 81.

4. Sylvie Fogiel-Bijaoui, "From Revolution to Motherhood: The Case of Women in the Kibbutz, 1910–1948." In *Pioneers and Homemakers*, edited by Deborah Bernstein (Albany: State Univ. of New York Press, 1992), 211–33.

5. The *kvutza* laid the ideological and structural foundations for the development of the *kibbutz* in the 1920s. The *kibbutz* is, a larger social unit with one hunderd or more members; the *kvotza* often restricted its membership to twenty or thirty. See Fogiel-Bijaoui, "From Revolution to Motherhood"; and Izraeli, "The Women's Workers' Movement."

6. Izraeli, "The Women's Workers' Movement."

7. Ibid., 205.

8. Ibid., 188.

9. Ibid, 204–06.

10. Fogiel-Bijaoui, "From Revolution to Motherhood," 215.

11. Ibid.

12. Ibid, 216.

13. For more material on women's struggles during this period, see Bernstein, *The Struggle for Equality*; Sylvie Fogiel-Bijaoui, *Revolution to Maternity: A Sociological History of the Condition of Women in the Kibbutz, 1910–1986*, (Hebrew), (Tel Aviv: Everyman University, 1993); Dafna Izraeli, "The Zionist Women's Movement in Palestine, 1911–1927: A Sociological Analysis," *Signs* 7 (1981): 87–114; and Bernstein, *Pioneers and Homemakers*.

14. The Hebrew translation is by the present author.

15. Natalie Rein, *Daughters of Rachel: Women in Israel* (New York: Penguin, 1980), 69.

16. For more detailed accounts of this period and of the influence of both Ben Gurion and Moshe Dayan in Israeli society and politics, see the appropriately titled Amos Elon, *The Israelis—Fathers and Sons* (London: Weidenfeld and Nicholson, 1971); Avraham Avihai, *Ben Gurion, State Builder, Principles and Pragmatism, 1948–1963* (Jerusalem: Israel Univ. Press, 1974); Noah Lucas, *The Modern History of Israel* (London: Weidenfeld and Nicholson, 1974); Shabtai Teveth, *Moshe Dayan* (London: Weidenfeld and Nicholson,1972) and Tom Segev, *1949: The First Israelis* (New York: Free Press, 1986).

17. Rein, 65.

18. David Ben Gurion, *Israel: A Personal History* (New York: Funk and Wagnalls, 1971), 8.

19. Ibid.

20. Chaim Hertzog, *The War of Atonement* (London: Weidenfeld and Nicholson, 1975), 2.

21. Rein, 75.

22. Nurit Gillath, 1991. "Women Against War: Parents Against Silence," in *Calling the Equality Bluff: Women in Israel*, ed. Barbara Swirski and Marilyn P. Safir (New York: Pergamon Press), 142–46.

23. Judith Buber Agassi, "How Much Political Power Do Israeli Women Have?" in *Calling the Equality Bluff: Women in Israel*, ed. Barbara Swirski and Marilyn P. Safir (New York: Pergamon Press, 1991), 203.

24. See Oriana Fallaci's interview with Golda Meir in her book, *Interviews with History* (Boston: Houghton Mifflin, 1976), 112.

25. Ibid.

26. See, for example, the special issues of the Israeli daily newspapers *Ma'ariv* and *Ydiot Achronot* commemorating the twentieth anniversary of the 1973 War, Sep. 24, 1993 (Hebrew).

27. See Dafna Sharfman, *Women and Politics*, (Tel Aviv: Tamar, 1988), 87–107; Rein, 87–93 and Freedman, 60–75.

28. Freedman, 68.

29. Ibid, 70–71.

30. *Women for a Renewed Society: The Newsletter of the Feminist Movement in Israel*, 4 (Sep. 1974), (Hebrew).

31. Pnina Krindel, "What Happened to the Israeli Women During the War?" *Women for a Renewed Society* 4: 14. Translation from Hebrew mine.

32. Ibid.

33. Ester Eilam, "Women and War," *Women for a Renewed Society* 4: 3.

34. This section draws primarily on Barbara Swirski's article, "Israeli Feminism New and Old," in *Calling the Equality Bluff: Women in Israel*, ed. Barbara Swirski and Marilyn P. Safir (New York: Pergamon Press, 1991), 294–302.

35. Ibid., 295. According to Barbara Swirski, the feminist organization in Tel Aviv resembled in its early years the American NOW or the French Choisire.

36. Ibid.

37. Ibid., 294.

38. Ibid., 296.

39. Ibid, 295; Rein, 95–96.

40. Rein, 95–96.

41. For a detailed account of the relationship between the CRM and the feminist movement and of Marcia Freedman's tenture as a Knesset Member, see Freedman, *Exile in the Promised Land*.

42. Ibid., 109.

43. The Women's Party Platform, Israel, 1977 (Hebrew).

44. Ibid.

45. Ibid.

46. Ibid.

47. For more about the political climate in Israel during that time, and the public's reaction to attempts to articulate connections between feminist politics and the Israeli-Palestinian conflict, see Freedman, 108.

48. The Women's Party Platform, Israel, 1977 (Hebrew).

49. See, for example, Sharfman; Swirski, "Israeli Feminism."

50. See Mordechi Bar-On, *Peace Now: The Portrait of a Movement* (Tel Aviv: Hkibbutz Hameuchad, 1985) (Hebrew); Reuven Kaminer, "The Protest Movement in Israel," in *Intifada: The Palestinian Uprising Against Israeli Occupation*, ed. Zachary Lockman and Joel Beinin (Boston: South End Press and MERIP,1989), 231–45; and Gadi Wolfsfeld, *The Politics of Provocation: Participation and Protest in Israel* (Albany: State Univ. of New York Press, 1988).

51. See Nurit Gillath, "The Thundering Silence: Parents Against Silence" (masters thesis. Univ. of Haifa, Haifa, Israel, 1987), (Hebrew) and Gillath, "Women Against War."

52. Quoted in Gillath, "The Thundering Silence," 142–43.

53. Ibid.

54. Ibid.

55. Wolfsfeld, 130.

56. Talhami, 15–27.

7. Israeli-Jewish Women and the *Intifada*

1. For detailed overviews of women's peace activism since the *intifada* see Naomi Chazan, "Israeli Women and Peace Activism," in *Calling the Equality Bluff: Women in Israel*, ed. Barbara Swirski and Marilyn Safir (New York: Pergamon Press, 1991) 152–64; Yvonne Deutsch, "Israeli Women: From Protest to a Culture of Peace," in *Walking the Red Line: Israelis in Search of Justice for Palestine*, ed. Deena Hurwitz (Philadelphia: New Society Publishers, 1991) and Sharoni, "Conflict Resolution.

2. Peace Now has generally supported the Labor Party's vague formulation of "territorial compromise" for peace, and has endorsed Shimon Peres's efforts to implement the Jordanian option—that is to establish a Palestinian state in the West Bank and Gaza Strip. In addition, although Peace Now recognized in principle the Palestinian people's right to self-determination, it has not demanded the establishment of an independent Palestinian state and has never advocated Israeli withdrawal from all

the territories occupied in 1967. Peace Now also echoed the national consensus in Israel on the question of Jerusalem by supporting annexation of the city and stressing the need to maintain its unified nature. For more on the responses of Peace Now and other groups of the Israeli left to the *intifada*, see Kaminer; and Stanley Cohen, "The *Intifada* in Israel: Potents and Precarious Balance," *Middle East Report*, 164–65 (May–Aug. 1990): 16–20.

3. Cohen, "The Intifada in Israel."

4. For more on the impact of the *intifada* on Israeli society, see Mordechai Bar-On, "Israeli Reactions to the Uprising," *Journal of Palestine Studies* 17 (Summer 1988): 46–65; Don Peretz, *Intifada: The Palestinian Uprising* (Boulder: Westview Press, 1990), 119–43; Azmy Bishara, "The Uprising's Impact on Israel," in *Intifada: The Palestinian Uprising Against Israeli Occupation*, ed. Zachary Lockman and Joel Beinin (Boston: South End Press and MERIP, 1989), 217–29; and Azmy Bishara, "The Third Factor: Impact of the *Intifada* on Israel," in *Intifada: Palestine at the Crossroads*, ed. Jamal Nassar and Roger Heacock (Birzeit University and Praeger, 1991), 271–86. On the mobilization of the Israeli peace movement during the *intifada*, see Edy Kaufman, "The *Intifada* and the Peace Camp in Israel," *Journal of Palestine Studies* 17 (Summer 1988): 66–81; Cohen, "The *Intifada* in Israel"; and Tamar Hermann, "The Israeli Peace Movement Confronted by the *Intifada* Challenge" (paper presented at the annual conference of the International Studies Association, Vancouver, Canada, March 1991).

5. Sharoni, "Conflict Resolution," 182.

6. Ibid.

7. Rachel Ostrowitz, "Dangerous Women: The Israeli Women's Peace Movement," *New Outlook* 32, nos. 6/7 (1989):14.

8. Ibid.

9. Sharoni, "Conflict Resolution," 185.

10. Ibid., 186–87.

11. Ibid., 188–94.

12. See also Rosenwasser, 105–28.

13. Sharoni, "Conflict Resolution," 314–25.

14. Rosenwasser, 106.

15. Sharoni, "Conflict Resolution," 195–99.

16. See SHANI's publication, "The Israeli-Palestinian Conflict: Questions and Answers," Jerusalem, 1989, 3 (Hebrew). The translation into English is mine.

17. During the first two years of the *intifada*, educational institutions, activities, teachers and students in the West Bank and Gaza Strip have been subjected to a series of repressive measures imposed by the military authorities. The four major universities, all institutions of higher education, as well as secondary and primary schools, have been closed for extended periods of time. The closure of schools was justified on security grounds. For more on this topic see Al-Haq, *Punishing A Nation: Human Rights Violations During the Palestinian Uprising, December 1987–1988*, 419–47.

18. *The Other Israel* 39 (Nov.–Dec. 1990): 8–9.

19. Sharoni, "Conflict Resolution," 244–50.

20. See Arela Daor's and Bilha Dvori's report from the conference in the Israeli daily *Davar*, 8 Dec. 1988 (Hebrew).

21. Press release, "Women and Peace," Jerusalem, June 1989.

22. Ibid.

23. Ibid.

24. Lily Galilee, "Rendezvous In Brussels," *New Outlook* 32, (June–July 1989): 27–29.

25. Project proposal: "The Jerusalem Link: A Women's Joint Venture for Peace," Jerusalem, 1992.

26. Ibid. See also Tikva Honig-Parnass, "Feminism and Peace Struggle in Israel," *News From Within* 10/11 (Oct.–Nov. 1992), 2.

27. Sharoni, "Conflict Resolution," 247–48.

28. Ibid.

29. Ibid., 171–79.

30. See Katia Azoulay G., "Elitism in the Women's Peace Movement," *Jerusalem Post*, 2 July 1989.

31. Sharoni, "Conflict Resolution," 235–58. See also Deutsch, "Towards a New Feminist Political Culture: Women Must Oppose the Principle of War," *Challenge* 2 (Mar.–Apr. 1991): 25–30; "Israeli Women: From Protest to a Culture of Peace," in *Walking the Red Line: Israelis in Search of Justice for Palestine,* ed. Deena Hurwitz, (Philadelphia, Pa: New Society Publishers, 1992), 46–55; and Erella Shadmi, "Politics Through the Back Door," *Women in Black National Newsletter,* 2 (Spring 1992): 7–9.

32. Sharoni, "Conflict Resolution," 235.

33. Ostrowitz, "Dangerous Women," 14–15.

34. Ibid.

35. Ibid.

36. Ibid.

37. For more on this particular case and for a theoretical discussion of the connections between militarism and sexism in the context of the Israeli-Palestinian conflict, see Sharoni "Every Woman is an Occupied Territory," and "Homefront as Battlefield."

38. *Hadashot,* 4 July 1991.

39. This information is based on the 1992 report of the WOFPP. For a detailed discussion of this case, see Sharoni, "Homefront as Battlefield." For more on sexual harassment and sexual violence suffered by Palestinian women at the hands of the Israeli military, see Nadira Shalhoub-Kevorkian, "Fear of Sexual Harassment: Palestinian Adolescent Girls in the *Intifada,*" in *Palestinian Women: Identity and Experience,* ed. Ebba Augustin (London: Zed Books, 1993), 171–80. See also "Political Detainees in the Russian Compound in Jerusalem: Overview and Testimonies Collected by the Women's Organization for Women Political Prisoners in Jerusalem," in *Augustin,* 185–97; and Rosenwasser, 112.

40. Sharoni, "Conflict Resolution," 236–38. See also Ostrowitz, 14–15.

41. Interview in Sharoni, "Conflict Resolution," 237.

42. Ibid.

43. Ibid.

44. Ibid, 169. The translation of the original press release into English is mine.

45. Ibid.

46. See Stanley Cohen, "From the Sealed Room: Israel's Peace Movement During the Gulf War," in *Beyond The Storm: A Gulf War Crisis Reader,* ed. Phyllis Bennis

and Michael Moushabeck (New York: Olive Branch Press, 1991), 205–14; and Mordechai Bar-On, "Israel and the Gulf War: A View from the Israeli Peace Movement," *Beyond The Storm*, 215–27.

47. Deutsch, "Israeli Women," 52–53.

48. Sharoni, "Conflict Resolution," 248–49.

49. Ibid, 171–72; and Alice Shalvi, "Violence Against Women Increases," *Challenge* 11 (Jan.–Feb. 1992): 31.

50. Sharoni, "Every Woman is an Occupied Territory," 459.

51. For a more detailed examination of the crisis in the women's peace movement following the 1991 Madrid conference see Simona Sharoni, "Search for a New Feminist Discourse," 22–23.

52. For a discussion of the implications of the September 1993 signing of the Declaration of Principles on the women's peace movement in Israel, especially on Women in Black in Jerusalem, see Ruth Cohen, "Women in Black Step Down," *Challenge* 22 (Nov.–Dec. 1993): 11–13.

53. Ibid., 11.

54. Ibid.

55. See Maxine Kaufman-Nunn, "What's New on the Peace Front: November 20–January 4," *Challenge* 23 (Jan.–Feb. 1994): 32.

56. *Challenge*, No. 26 (July–Aug. 1994), 29.

57. See, for example, Honig-Parnass, 2–5; and Erella Shadmi, "Women, Palestinians, Zionism: A Personal View," *News From Within* 10/11 (Oct.–Nov. 1992): 13–16.

8. The Politics of Alliances Between Palestinian and Israeli Women

1. For an extensive discussion of this point, see Young, 75–157.

2. Ibid., 77.

3. Young's book reflects this tendency.

4. See, for example, Kandiyoti, "Identity and Its Discontents"; and Yuval-Davis and Anthias.

5. See Young, 138; and Rachel Katznelson-Shazar, ed. *The Plough Woman: Memoirs of the Pioneer Women of Palestine* (New York: Herzl Press, 1975), 121.

6. Ada Maimon, *Women Build a Land* (New York: Herzl Press, 1962), 76.

7. Ibid.

8. Young, 138.

9. Ibid., 148–49.

10. Sharoni, "Conflict Resolution," 308–09.

11. Talhami, 23.

12. Ibid.

13. Ibid.

14. Ibid.

15. Sharoni, "Conflict Resolution," 241–55.

16. Interview, May 1990, Tel Aviv, Israel

17. Ibid.

18. Abdo, "Women of the *Intifada*," 25.

19. Ibid.

20. Ibid., 25–26.

21. It was pointed out in a recently published anthology on dialogue and the Israeli-Palestinian conflict that "if asked, many people are likely to say that dialogue is good. It has been linked to 'motherhood and apple pie,' something which no one would publicly reject." See Haim Gordon and Rivka Gordon, eds., *Israel/Palestine: The Quest for Dialogue* (New York: Orbis, 1991), 2.

22. This account is based on my participation in the dialogue encounter in Jenin, June 1990, Occupied East Bank.

23. There is very little published about this group; those who are interested in more information should contact Bracha Yanuv, one of its founding members at the following address: Tor Hazahav Street, Herzelia, Israel.

24. Symbols associated with motherhood were used primarily in the context of nonviolent women's resistance. There has been a tendency to interpret the connections between motherhood and peace as evidence that women are inherently more peaceful than men because of their ability to give life, nurture, and care. At the same time, there are women (and men) who call into question the simplistic equation of men with war and women or mothers with peace, but nevertheless find the images of motherhood politically useful in particular contexts. See, for example, Sara Ruddick, *Maternal Thinking: Toward a Politics of Peace* (New York: Ballantine Books, 1989); and "Mothers and Men's Wars," in *Rocking the Ship of State: Toward a Feminist Peace Politics*, ed. Adrienne Harris and Ynestra King (Boulder, Colo.: Westview Press, 1989), 75–92. See also Marysa Navarro, "The Personal is Political: Las Madres de Plaza Mayo," in *Power and Popular Protest: Latin American Social Movements*, ed. Susan Eckstein (Berkeley: Univ. of California Press, 1989); Alonso, *Peace as a Women's Issue*, (Syracuse: Syracuse Univ. Press, 1993); and Amy Swerdlow, *Women Strike for Peace: Traditional Motherhood and Radical Politics in the 1960s* (Chicago: Univ. of Chicago Press, 1993).

25. Cited in Sharoni, "Conflict Resolution," 230.

26. Mohammed Abu-Nimer, "Conflict Resolution Between Arabs and Jews in Israel: A Study of Six Intervention Models" (Ph.D. diss., George Mason Univ., 1993), 1.

27. Personal conversation, June 1991, Ramallah, Occupied West Bank.

28. Ibid.

29. Ibid, 28.

30. Interview, May 1990, Tel Aviv, Israel.

31. Ibid.

32. Sharoni, "Conflict Resolution," 328.

33. Personal conversation, June 1991, Ramallah, Occupied West Bank.

34. Ibid.

35. Deutsch, " Israeli Women," 49.

36. Ibid.

37. Ibid.

38. Harding, 288–95.

9. Conclusion

1. Enloe, *Bananas, Beaches and Bases*, 201.
2. Kathy Furguson, *The Man Question: Visions of Subjectivity in Feminist Theory* (Berkeley: Univ. of California Press, 1993).
3. Cohn, 64.

Bibliography

Abdo, Nahla. *Family, Women and Social Change in the Middle East: The Palestinian Case*. Toronot: Scholars Press, 1987.

———. "Middle East Politics Through Feminist Lenses: Negotiating the Terms of Solidarity," *Alternatives* 18 (1993): 29–38.

———. "Women of the *Intifada*: Gender, Class and National Liberation," *Race & Class* 32, no. 4, (1991): 19–34.

Abou-Zeid, Ahmed. "Honor and Shame Among the Bedouins of Egypt." In *Honor and Shame: The Values of Mediterranean Society*, edited by J. G. Peristiany. Chicago: Univ. of Chicago Press, 1966.

Abu-Lughud, Lila. *Veiled Sentiments: Honor and Poetry in a Bedouin Society*. Berkeley: Univ. of California Press, 1986.

Abu-Nimer, Mohammed. "Conflict Resolution Between Arabs and Jews in Israel: A Study of Six Intervention Models." Ph.D. diss. George Mason Univ., 1993.

Afshar, Haleh, ed. *Women in the East: Perceptions, Realities, and Struggles for Liberation*. New York: St. Martins's Press, 1992.

Ahmed, Leila. "Feminism and Feminist Movements in the Middle East." In *Women and Islam*, edited by Aziz al-Hibri, 153–68. New York: Pergamon Press, 1982.

———. *Women and Gender in Islam: Historical Roots of a Modern Debate*. New Haven: Yale Univ. Press, 1992.

Alonso, Harriet Hyman. *Peace as a Women's Issue: A History of the U.S. Movement for World Peace and Women's Rights*. Syracuse: Syracuse Univ. Press, 1993.

Altorki, Soraya and Camillia Fawzi Ei-Solh, eds. *Arab Women in the Field: Studying Your Own Society*. Syracuse: Syracuse Univ. Press, 1988.

Anderson, Benedict. *Imagined Communities: Reflections on the Origins and Spread of Nationalism*. London: Verso, 1983.

Antonius, Soraya. "Fighting on Two Fronts: Conversations with Palestinian Women." *Journal of Palestine Studies* 31 (Spring 1979): 26–45.

Anzaldua, Gloria. *Borderlands/La Frontera: The New Mestiza.* San Francisco: Aunt Lute Books, 1987.

Aruri, Naseer, ed. *Occupation: Israel Over Palestine.* 2nd ed. Belmont, Mass.: Association of Arab-American Univ. Graduates, 1989.

Ashrawi, Hanan Mikhail. "The Other Occupation: The Palestinian Response." In *Beyond the Storm: A Gulf Crisis Reader,* edited by Phyllis Bennis and Michel Moushabeck, 191–98. New York: Olive Branch Press, 1991.

Augustin, Ebba, ed. *Palestinian Women: Identity and Experience.* London: Zed Books, 1993.

Avihai, Avraham. *Ben Gurion, State Builder, Principles and Pragmatism, 1948–1963.* Jerusalem: Israel Univ. Press, 1974.

Azmon, Yael and Dafna N. Israeli, eds. *Women in Israel.* New Brunswick, Transaction, 1993.

Azoulay-Gibel, Katia. "Elitism in the Women's Peace Movement." *The Jerusalem Post* 2 July 1989.

Badran, Margot. "Dual Liberation: Feminism and Nationalism in Egypt, 1870s–1925." *Feminist Issues* (Spring 1988): 15–34.

———. "Dual Liberation and Independent Women: More Than a Century of Feminism in Egypt." in *Arab Women: Old Boundaries, New Frontiers,* edited by Judith Tucker, 195–207. Bloomington: Indiana Univ. Press, 1993.

Badran, Margot and Miriam Cooke, eds. *Opening the Gates: A Century of Arab Feminist Writing.* Bloomington: Indiana Univ. Press, 1990.

Bar-On, Mordechai. "Israel and the Gulf War: A View from the Israeli Peace Movement." In *Beyond the Storm: A Gulf Crisis Reader,* edited by Phyllis Bennis and Michel Moushabeck, 215–27. New York: Olive Branch Press, 1991.

———. "Israeli Reactions to the Uprising." *Journal of Palestine Studies* 17 (Summer 1988): 46–65.

———. *Peace Now: The Portrait of a Movement.* Tel Aviv: Hkibbutz Hameuchad, 1985 (Hebrew).

Beck, Lois and Nikki R. Keddie, eds. *Women in the Muslim World.* Cambridge, Mass.: Harvard Univ. Press, 1978.

Ben Gurion, David. *Israel: A Personal History.* New York: Funk and Wagnalls, 1971.

Bernstein, Deborah. "In Search of a New Female Identity: Pioneering Women in Prestate Israeli Society." *Shofar: An Interdisciplinary Journal of Jewish Studies* 9, no. 4 (Summer 1991): 78–91.

———. *The Struggle for Equality: Urban Women Workers in Prestate Israeli Society.* New York: Praeger, 1987.

Beth, Amy. "Women Struggle for Peace in a Time of Crisis." *Bridges* 2, no. 1 (Spring 1991): 81–83.

Bishara, Azmy. "The Third Factor: Impact of the Intifada on Israel." In *Intifada: Palestine at the Crossroads*, edited by Jamal Nassar and Roger Heacock, 271–86. Birzerb Univ. Praeger, 1991.

————. "The Uprising's Impact on Israel." In *The Palestinian Uprising Against Israeli Occupation*, edited by Zachary Lockman and Joel Beinin, 217–19. Boston: South End Press, 1989.

Bloom, Anne. "The Third Factor: Impact of the *Intifada* on Israel." In *Intifada: Palestine at the Crossroads* edited by Jamal Nassar and Roger Heacock, 271–86. New York: Birzeit University and Praeger, 1991.

————. "Women in the Defense Force." In *Calling the Equality Bluff: Women in Israel* edited by Barbara Swirski and Marilyn Safir, 128–38. New York: Pergamon Press, 1991.

Bourne, Jenny. "Homelands of the Mind: Jewish Feminism and Identity Politics." *Race & Class* 19 (1987): 1–24.

Brown, Wendy. *Manhood and Politics*. Totawa, N.J.: Rowman and Littlefield, 1988.

Buber-Agassi, Judith. "How Much Political Power Do Israeli Women Have?" In *Calling the Equality Bluff: Women in Israel*, edited by Barbara Swirski and Marilyn Safir, 319–27. New York: Pergamon Press, 1991.

Butler, Judith. *Gender Trouble: Feminism and the Subversion of Identity*. New York: Routledge, 1990.

Butler, Judith and Joan W. Scott, eds. *Feminists Theorize the Political*. New York: Routledge, 1992.

Campbell, David. *Writing Security: United States Foreign Policy and the Politics of Identity*. Minneapolis: Univ. of Minnesota Press, 1992.

Challenge 26 (July–Aug. 1994): 29.

Challenge, "Closure." May–June 1993.

Challenge, "Gaza and Jericho—First or Last?" Sept.–Oct. 1993.

Chazan, Naomi. "Israeli Women and Peace Activism." In *Calling the Equality Bluff: Women in Israel*, edited by Barbara Swirski and Marilyn Safir, 152–64. New York: Pergamon Press, 1991.

Chow, Rey. "Violence in the Other Country: China as Crisis, Spectacle, and Woman." In *Third World Women and the Politics of Feminism*, edited by Chandra T. Mohanty, Ann Russo and Lourdes Torres, Bloomington: Indiana Univ. Press, 1991.

Cobban, Helena. *The Palestinian Liberation Organization: People, Power and Politics*. Cambridge Univ. Press, 1984.

Cohen, Ruth. "Women in Black Step Down." *Challenge* 22 (Nov.–Dec. 1993): 11–13.

Cohen, Stanley. "From the Sealed Room: Israel's Peace Movement During the Gulf War." In *Beyond the Storm: A Gulf Crisis Reader*, edited by Phyllis

Bennis and Michel Moushabeck, 205–14. New York: Olive Branch Press, 1991.

———. "The Intifada in Israel: Potents and Precarious Balance." *Middle East Report* 164–65 (May–Aug. 1990): 16–20.

Cohn, Carol. "Sex and Death in the Rational World of Defense Intellectuals." In *Peace: Meanings, Politics, Strategies,* edited by Linda Rennie Forcey, 39–72. New York: Praeger, 1989.

Combs-Schilling, Eillain M. *Sacred Performances: Islam, Sexuality and Sacrifice.* New York: Columbia Univ. Press, 1989.

Dajani, Souad. "Palestinian Women Under Israeli Occupation: Implications for Development." In *Arab Women: Old Boundaries, New Frontiers,* edited by Judith Tucker, 149–53. Bloomington: Indiana Univ. Press, 1993.

Davar 8 Dec. 1988 (Hebrew).

Davies, Miranda, ed. *Third World-Second Sex: Women's Struggles and National Liberation.* London: Zed Books, 1983.

Deutsch, Yvonne. "Israeli Women: From Protest to a Culture of Peace." In *Walking the Red Line: Israelis in Search of Justice for Palestine,* edited by Deena Hurwitz, Philadelphia: New Society, 1992, 46–55.

———. "Towards a New Feminist Political Culture: Women Must Oppose the Principle of War." *Challenge* 2, no. 2 (1991): 25–30.

Diamond, Irene and Gloria Feman Orenstein, eds., *Reweaving the World: The Emergence of Ecofeminism.* San Francisco: Sierra Club Books, 1990.

Eilam, Ester. "Women and War." *Women for a Renewed Society: The Newsletter of the Feminist Movement in Israel* 4 (Sept. 1974): 3.

Elon, Amos. *The Israelis—Fathers and Sons.* London: Weidenfeld and Nicholson, 1971.

Enloe, Cynthia H. *Bananas, Beaches and Bases: Making Feminist Sense of International Politics.* Berkeley: Univ. of California Press, 1989.

———. *Does Khaki Become You? The Militarization of Women's Lives.* London: Pluto Press, 1983.

———. *The Morning After: Sexual Politics at the End of the Cold War.* Berkeley: Univ. of California Press, 1993.

al-Fajar-Jerusalem Palestinian Weekly, 8 March 1985.

Fallaci, Oriana. *Interviews with History.* Boston: Houghton Mifflin, 1976.

Ferguson Kathy. *The Man Question: Visions of Subjectivity in Feminist Theory.* Berkeley: Univ. of California Press, 1993.

Fernea, Elizabeth and Basima Bezirgan, eds. *Middle East Muslim Women Speak.* Austin: Univ. of Texas Press, 1977.

Flax, Jane. "Postmodernism and Gender Relations in Feminist Theory." In *Feminism/Postmodernism,* edited by Linda Nicholson, 39–62. New York: Routledge, 1989.

Fogiel-Bijaoui, Sylvie. "From Revolution to Motherhood: The Case of Women in the Kibbutz, 1910–1948." In *Pioneers and Homemakers*, edited by Deborah Bernstein, 211–33. Albany: State Univ. of New York Press, 1992.

————. *Revolution to Maternity: A Sociological History of the Condition of Women in the Kibbutz, 1910–1986*. Tel Aviv: Everyman Univ., 1993 (Hebrew).

Freedman, Marcia. *Exile in the Promised Land: A Memoir*. New York: Firebrand Books, 1990.

Galilee, Lily. "Rendezvous in Brussels." *New Outlook* 32 (June–July 1989): 27–29.

Geiger, H. Jack, Jennifer Leaning, Leon A. Shapiro, and Bennett Simon. *The Casualities of Conflict: Medical Care and Human Rights in the West Bank and Gaza Strip*. Sometville, Mass.: Physicians for Human Rights, 1988.

Ghossoub, Mai. "A Reply to Hammami and Reiker." *New Left Review* 20 (1988): 8–11.

Giacaman, Rita, "Reflections on the Palestinian Women's Movement in the Israeli Occupied Territories." Unpublished manuscript, Birzeit Univ., West Bank, May 1987.

————. "An Uneasy Peace in the Middle East for a Palestinian." *Ms.* (Jan.–Feb. 1994): 10.

Giacaman, Rita and Penny Johnson. "Palestinian Women: Building Barricades and Breaking Barriers." In *Intifada: The Palestinian Uprising Against Israeli Occupation*, edited by Zachary Lockman and Joel Beinin, 155–170. Boston: South End Press and MERIP, 1989.

————. "Searching for Strategies: The Palestinian Women's Movement in the New Era." *Middle East Report* 186 (Jan.–Feb. 1994): 22–26.

Gillath, Nurit. "The Thundering Silence: Parents Against Silence." Master's thesis, Univ. of Haifa, Haifa, Israel, 1987 (Hebrew).

————. "Women Against War: Parents Against Silence," In *Calling the Equality Bluff: Women in Israel*, edited by Barbara Swirski and Marilyn P. Safir, 142–46. New York: Pergamon Press, 1991.

Glavanis, Kathy. "The Women's Movement, Feminism, and the National Struggles in Palestine: Unresolved Contradictions." *Journal of Gender Studies* 1, no. 4 (1992): 463–74.

Gordon, Haim and Rivka Gordon, eds. *Israel/Palestine: The Quest for Dialogue*. New York: Orbis, 1991.

Gorelick, Sherry. "Geneva Conference: History and Goals." *Jewish Women's Peace Bulletin*, May 1991:3.

Hadashot, 4 July 1991.

Haj, Samira. "Palestinian Women and Patriarchal Relations." *Signs: Journal of Women in Culture and Society* 17, no. 4 (Summer 1992): 761–78.

Hajibashi, Zjaleh. "Feminism or Ventriloquism: Western Presentations of Middle Eastern Women." *Middle East Report* 172 (1991): 43–5.

Halaileh, Samir. "The Gulf Crisis and the Economy in the Occupied Territories." In *Beyond the Storm: A Gulf Crisis Reader,* edited by Phyllis Bennis and Michgel Moushabeck, 199–204. New York: Olive Branch Press, 1991.

Hammami, Rema. "The Role of the Woman on the Levels of Politics and the Struggle in the Intifada: A Critical Approach." Paper presented at the "The Intifada and Some Women's Social Issues" conference, Ramallah, Occupied West Bank, Dec. 1990.

————. "Women, the Hijab, and the Intifada." *Middle East Report* 164/165 (1990): 24–31.

Hammami, Rema and Martin Rieker, "Feminist Orientalism and Orientalist Marxism," *New Left Review* 20 (1988): 1–7.

al-Haq (Law in the Service of Man). *Punishing a Nation: Human Rights Violations During the Uprising, Dec. 1987–Dec. 1988.* Boston: South End Press, 1990.

Haraway, Donna. "Situated Knowledge: The Science Question in Feminism and the Privilege of Partial Perspective." *Feminist Studies* 14, no. 3 (1988): 575–99.

Harding, Sandra. *Whose Science? Whose Knowledge? Thinking from Women's Lives.* New York: Cornell Univ. Press, 1991.

Harris, Adrienne and Ynestra King, eds. *Rockinig the Ship of State: Toward a Feminist Peace Politics.* Boulder: Westview Press, 1989.

Hatem, Mervet. "Toward the Development of Post-Islamist and Post-Nationalist Feminist Discourses in the Middle East." In *Arab Women: Old Boundaries, New Frontiers,* edited by Judith Tucker, 29–48. Bloomington: Indiana Univ. Press.

Hazleton, Lesely. *Israeli Women: The Reality Behind the Myths.* New York: Simon and Schuster, 1977.

Hermann, Tamar. "The Israeli Peace Movement Confronted by the Intifada Challenge." Paper presented at the annual conference of the International Studies Association, Vancouver, Canada, March 1991.

Hertzog, Chaim. *The War of Atonement.* London: Weidenfeld and Nicholson, 1975.

Hiltermann, Joost. *Behind the Intifada: Labor and Women's Movements in the Occupied Territories.* Princeton: Princeton Univ. Press, 1991.

Hindiye, Suha and Afaf Ghazawneh. "The Socio-economic Conditions of Female Wage Labour in the West Bank." In *Palestinian Women: Identity and Experience,* edited by Ebba Augustin, 66–75. London: Zed Books, 1993.

Honig-Parnass, Tikva. "Feminism and Peace Struggle in Israel." *News From Within* 10/11 (Oct.–Nov. 1992): 2–5.

hooks, bell. *Talking Back: Thinking Feminist, Thinking Black*. Boston: South End Press, 1989.

Hull, Gloria P., Patricia Scott, and Barbara Smith, eds. *But Some of Us Are Brave*. New York: Feminist Press, 1982.

Huston, Perdita. *Third World Women Speak Out*. New York: Praeger, 1979.

Ismail, Noha S. "The Palestinian Women's Struggle for Independence: A Historical Perspective." In *The Third Wave: Feminist Perspectives on Racism*, edited by Jacqui Alexander, Lisa Albrecht, Sharon Day, Mab Segrest, and Norma Alarcon. New York: Kitchen Table: Woman of Color Press, 1993.

Izraeli, Dafna. "The Women's Workers' Movement: First Wave Feminism in Pre-State Israel." In *Pioneers and Homemakers: Jewish Women in Pre-State Israel*, edited by Deborah Bernstein. Albany: State Univ. of New York Press, 1992.

———. "The Zionist Women's Movement in Palestine, 1911–1927: A Sociological Analysis." *Signs: Journal of Women in Culture and Society* 7 (1981): 87–114.

Jad, Islah. "From Salons to the Popular Committees: Palestinian Women, 1919–1989. In *Intifada: Palestine at the Crossroads*, edited by Jamal R. Nassar and Roger Heacock. New York: Birzeit Univ. and Praeger Publishers, 1990.

Jammal, Laila. *Contributions by Palestinian Women to the National Struggle for Liberation*. Washington, D.C.: Middle East Public Relations, 1985.

Jayawardena, Kumari. *Feminism and Nationalism in the Third World*. London: Zed Press Ltd., 1986.

Jerusalem Media and Communication Center, Weekly Report, 11–17 July 1993.

Joseph, Suad. "Women and Politics in the Middle East." *Middle East Report* 138 (Jan.–Feb. 1986): 3–7.

Journal of Palestine Studies 70 (Winter 1989): 213–23.

Kaminer, Reuven. "The Protest Movement in Israel." In *Intifada: The Palestinian Uprising Against Israeli Occupation*, edited by Zachary Lockman and Joel Beinin, 231–45. Boston: South End Press and MERIP, 1989.

Kandiyoti, Deniz. "Identity and Its Discontents: Women and the Nation." *Millennium: Journal of International Studies* 20, no. 3 (1991): 429–43.

———. "Strategies for Feminist Scholarship in the Middle East." Paper presented at the 27th Annual Meeting of the Middle East Studies Association (MESA), Research Triangle Park, North Carolina, Nov. 1993.

———. *Women, Islam and the State*. Philadelphia: Temple Univ. Press, 1991.

Katznelson-Shazar, Rachel. *The Plough Woman: Memoirs of the Pioneer Women of Palestine*. New York: Herzl Press, 1975.

Kaufman, Edy. "The Intifada and the Peace Camp in Israel." *Journal of Palestine Studies* 17 (Summer 1988): 66–81.

Kaufman-Nunn, Maxine. "What's New on the Peace Front: November 20–January 4." *Challenge* 23 (Jan.–Feb. 1994): 32.

Keddie, Nikki R. and Beth Baron, eds. *Women in Middle Eastern History: Shifting Boundaries in Sex and Gender*. New Haven: Yale Univ. Press, 1991.

Khaled, Leila. *My People Shall Live: The Autobiography of a Revolutionary*. London: Hodder and Stoughton, 1973.

al-Khayyat, Sana. *Honor and Shame: Women in Modern Iraq*. London: Saqi Books, 1990.

Krindel, Pnina. "What Happened to the Israeli Women During the War?" *Women for a Renewed Society: The Newsletter of the Feminist Movement in Israel* 4–5 (1974) (Hebrew).

Kuttab, Eileen. "The *Intifada* and some Women's Social Issues." Paper presented at the Bisan Research and Development Center, Occupied East Jerusalem, December 1990.

Lather, Patti. *Getting Smart: Feminist Research and Pedagogy Within the Postmodern*. New York: Routledge, 1991.

Layoun, Mary. "Telling Spaces: Palestinian Women and The Engendering of National Narratives." In *Nationalisms & Sexualities*, edited by Andrew Parker et al., 407–23. New York: Routledge, 1992.

Lazreg, Marnia. "Feminism and Difference: The Perils of Writing as a Woman on Women in Algeria." In *Conflicts in Feminism*, edited by Marianne Hirsch and Evelyn Fox-Keller, 326–48. New York: Routledge, 1990.

Lindsay, Beverly. ed. *Comparative Perspectives of Third World Women: The Impact of Race, Sex and Class*. New York: Praeger, 1983.

Lipman, Beita. *Israel: The Embattled Land—Jewish and Palestinian Women Talk About Their Lives*. London: Pandora, 1988.

Lucas, Noah. *The Modern History of Israel*. London: Weidenfeld and Nicholson, 1974.

Ma'ariv, 3 Sept. 1993, 4–5 (Hebrew).

Ma'ariv, 24 Sept. 1993. Special supplement (Hebrew).

Mabro, Judy. *Veiled Half Truths: Western Travellers' Perceptions of Middle Eastern Women*. New York: St. Martin's Press, 1991.

MacLeod, Arlene Elowe. *Accommodating Protest: Working Women, the New Veiling and Change in Cairo*. New York: Columbia Univ. Press, 1991.

———. "Hegemonic Relations and Gender Resistance: The New Veiling as Accommodating Protest in Cairo." *Signs* (1992): 533–57.

Maimon, Ada. *Women Build a Land*. New York: Herzl Press, 1962.

Mernissi, Fatima. *Beyond the Veil: Male-Female Dynamics in a Modern Muslim Society*. New York: John Wiley, 1975.

Middle East Report. "After Oslo: The Shape of Palestine to Come." 186 (Jan.–Feb. 1994).

Middle East Watch. *The Israeli Army and the Intifada: Policies That Contribute to the Killings*. New York: Human Rights Watch, 1990.

Minces, Juliette. *The House of Obedience: Women in Arab Society*. London: Zed Books, 1980.

Mogannam, Mateil. *The Arab Woman and the Palestine Problem*. London: Herbert Joseph, 1937. Reprinted: Westport, Conn.: Hyperion Press, 1976.

Moghadam, Valentine M. *Gender and National Identity: Women and Politics in Muslim Societies*. London: Zed Books, 1994.

———. *Modernizing Women: Gender and Social Change in the Middle East*. Boulder: Lynne Rienner Publishers, 1993.

Mohanty, Chandra T. "Cartographies of Struggle: Third World Women and the Politics of Feminism." In *Third World Women and the Politics of Feminism*, edited by Chandra T. Mohanty, Ann Russo and Lourdes Torres, 1–47. Bloomington: Indiana Univ. Press, 1991.

———. "Feminist Encounters: Locating the Politics of Experience." In *Destabilizing Theory: Contemporary Feminist Debates*, edited by Michele Barrett and Anne Phillips, 74–92. Stanford: Stanford Univ. Press, 1992.

———. "Under Western Eyes: Feminist Scholarship and Colonial Discourses." In *Third World Women and the Politics of Feminism*, edited by Chandra T. Mohanty, Ann Russo and Lourdes Torres, 51–80. Bloomington: Indiana Univ. Press, 1991.

Mohanty, Chandra T. and Biddy Martin. "Feminist Politics: What's Home Got To Do With It?" In *Feminist Studies/Critical Studies*, edited by Teresa de Lauretis, 191–212. Bloomington: Indiana Univ. Press, 1986.

Moraga, Cherrie and Gloria Anzaldua, eds. *This Bridge Called My Back: Writings By Radical Women of Color*. New York: Kitchen Table: Woman of Color Press, 1983.

Morgan, Robin, ed. *Sisterhood is Powerful: An Anthology of Writings from the Women's Liberation Movement*. New York: Vintage, 1970.

Najjar, Orayb Aref with Kitty Warnock. *Portraits of Palestinian Women*. Salt Lake City: Univ. of Utah Press, 1992.

Najmabadi, Afsaneh. "Hazards of Modernity and Morality: Women, State and Ideology in Contemporary Iran." In *Women, Islam and the State* edited by Deniz Kandiyoti, 48–76. Philadelphia: Temple University Press, 1991.

———. "Iran's Turn to Islam: From Modernism to a Moral Order." *The Middle East Journal* 41, no. 2 (1987): 202–17.

Navarro, Marysa. "The Personal is Political: Las Madres de Plaza Mayo." In *Power and Popular Protest: Latin American Social Movements*, edited by Susan Eckstein, 241–59. University of California Press, 1989.

Nelson, Cynthia. "Public and Private Politics: Women in the Middle Eastern World." *American Ethnologist* 1 (Aug. 1974): 551–63.

News From Within, Jan.–Feb. 1993.

New York Times, 14 Sept. 1993, sec. 1.

New York Times, 3 Feb. 1994, sec. 1.

Niva, Steve. "The Battle is Joined." In *Beyond the Storm: A Gulf Crisis Reader*, edited by Phyllis Bennis and Michel Moushabeck, 55–71. New York: Olive Branch Press, 1991.

Opie, Anne. "Qualitative Research, Appropriation of the 'Other' and Empowerment." *Feminist Review* 3 (1991): 52–69.

Ostrowitz, Rache. "Dangerous Women: The Israeli Women's Peace Movement." *New Outlook* 32, nos. 6/7 (1989): 14–15.

Peretz, Don. *Intifada: The Palestinian Uprising*. Boulder: Westview Press, 1990.

Peteet, Julie. *Gender in Crisis: Women and the Palestinian Resistance Movement*. New York: Columbia Univ. Press, 1991.

Peterson, V. Spike. ed. *Gendered States: Feminist (Re) Visions Of International Relations Theory*. Boulder: Lynne and Rienner, 1992.

Peterson, V. Spike and Anne Sisson Runyan. *Global Gender Issues*. Boulder: Westview Press, 1993.

Pratt, Minnie Bruce. "Identity: Skin, Blood, Heart." In *Yours in Struggle: Three Feminist Perspectives on Anti-Semitism and Racism*, edited by Elly Bulkin, Minnie Bruce Pratt and Barbara Smith, 9–63. New York: Firebrand Books, 1984.

Rein, Natalie. *Daughters of Rachel: Women in Israel*. New York: Penguin, 1980.

Reshet, "The Jerusalem Link: A Women's Joint Venture for Peace." Jerusalem, 1992.

Rockwell, Susan. "Palestinian Women Workers in the Israeli-Occupied Gaza Strip." *Journal of Palestine Studies* 14, no. 2 (Winter 1985): 114–36.

Rodda, Annabel. *Women and the Environment*. London: Zed Books, 1991.

Rosaldo, Michelle. "Woman, Culture and Society: A Theoretical Overview." In *Woman, Culture and Society*, edited by Michelle Rosaldo, 17–42. Stanford: Stanford Univ. Press, 1974.

Rosenwasser, Penny. *Voices from a Promised Land: Palestinian and Israeli Peace Activists Speak Their Hearts*. Willimantic, Conn.: Curbstone Press, 1992.

Ruddick, Sara. *Maternal Thinking: Toward a Politics of Peace*. New York: Ballantine Books, 1989.

———. "Mothers and Men's Wars." In *Rocking the Ship of State: Toward a Feminist Peace Politics*, edited by Adrienne Harris and Ynestra King, 75–92. Boulder: Westview Press, 1989.

Sabbagh, Suha. "Palestinian Women Writers and the *Intifada,*" *Social Text* 22 (1989): 1–19.

Sabbagh, Suha and Ghada Talhami, eds. *Images and Reality: Palestinian Women under Occupation and in the Diaspora.* Washington D.C.: Institute of Arab Women's Studies, 1990.

Said, Edward. "The Burdens of Interpretation and the Question of Palestine." *Journal of Palestine Studies* 16, no. 1 (Autumn 1986): 29–37.

———. *Orientalism.* New York: Vintage, 1979.

Sayigh, Rosemary. "Encounters with Palestinian Women under Occupation." *Journal of Palestine Studies* 40 no. 4 (Summer 1981): 3–26.

———. "Palestinian Women: A Case of Neglect." In *Portraits of Palestinian Women,* edited by Orayab Najjar with Kitty Warnock. Salt Lake City: Univ. of Utah Press, 1992.

———. *Palestinians: from Peasants to Revolutionaries.* London: Zed Books, 1979.

Sayigh, Rosemary and Julie Peteet, "Between Two Fires: Palestinian Women in Lebanon." In *Caught Up in Conflict: Women's Responses to Political Strife,* edited by Rosemary Ridd and Helen Callaway, 106–37. London: Macmillan Education, 1986.

Segev, Tom. *1949: The First Israelis.* New York: Free Press, 1986.

———. *The Seventh Million: The Israelis and the Holocaust.* Jerusalem: Maxwell-Macmillan-Keter, 1991 (Hebrew).

Shadmi, Erella, "Politics Through the Back Door." *Women in Black National Newsletter* 2 (Spring 1992): 7–9.

———. "Women, Palestinians, Zionism: A Personal View." *News From Within* 10/11 (Oct.–Nov. 1992): 13–16.

Shalhoub-Kevorkian, Nadira. "Fear of Sexual Harassment: Palestinian Adolescent Girls in the Intifada." In *Palestinian Women: Identity and Experience,* edited by Ebba Augustin, 171–80. London: Zed Books, 1993, 171–80.

Shalvi, Alice. "Violence Against Women Increases." *Challenge,* 11 (Jan.–Feb., 1992): 31.

Shani, "The Israeli-Palestinian Conflict: Questions and Answers." Jerusalem, 1989 (Hebrew).

Sharfman, Dafna. *Women and Politics.* Tel Aviv: Tamar, 1988 (Hebrew).

Sharoni, Simona. "Conflict Resolution through Feminist Lenses: Theorizing the Israeli-Palestinian Conflict from the Perspectives of Women Peace Activists in Israel." Ph.D. diss., George Mason Univ., 1993.

———. "Every Woman is an Occupied Territory: The Politics of Militarism and Sexism and the Israeli-Palestinian Conflict." *Journal of Gender Studies* 1, no. 4 (1992): 447–62.

———. "Homefront as Battlefield: Gender, Military Occupation and Violence Against Women." In *Women and the Israeli Occupation: The Politics of Change,* edited by Tamar Mayer, New York Routledge 1994.

———. "Is Feminism a Threat to National Security?" *Ms.* 3, no. 4 Jan./Feb. (1993): 18–22.

———. "Middle East Politics Through Feminist Lenses: Toward Theorizing International Relations from Women's Struggles." *Alternatives* 18, no. 1 (1993): 5–28.

Shiva, Vandana. *Staying Alive: Women, Ecology and Devepment.* London: Zed Books, 1989.

Smith, Barbara. *Home Girls: A Black Feminist Anthology.* New York: Kitchen Table: Woman of Color Press, 1983.

Sparks, December 1991.

Strum, Phillipa. *The Women Are Marching: The Second Sex and the Palestinian Revolution.* New York: Lawrence Hill Books, 1992.

Swedenburg, Ted. "Palestinian Women in the 1936–1939 Revolt: Implications for the Intifada." Paper presented at the "Marxism Now: Tradition and Difference" conference, Univ. of Massachusetts, Amherst, Dec. 1989.

Swerdlow, Amy. *Women Strike for Peace: Traditional Motherhood and Radical Politics in the 1960s.* Chicago: Univ. of Chicago Press, 1993.

Swirski, Barbara. "Israeli Feminism New and Old." In *Calling the Equality Bluff: Women in Israel,* edited by Barbara Swirski and Marilyn Safir, 285–302. New York: Pergamon Press, 1991.

Sylvester, Christine. "The Emperors' Theories and Transformations: Looking at the Field Through Feminist Lenses." In *Transformations in Global Political Economy,* edited by Dennis Piraga and Christine Sylvester, London: Macmillan, 1990.

Talhami, Ghada. "Women Under Occupation: The Great Transformation." In *Images and Reality: Palestinian Women Under Occupation,* edited by Suha Sabbagh and Ghada Talhami, 15–27. Washington D.C.: Institute for Arab Women's Studies, 1990.

Taraki, Lisa. "Women's Organizations in Palestine." In *Directory of Palestinian Women's Organizations,* edited by The Women's Studies Committee/ Bisan Center. Ramallah: Hussary Press, 1993.

Teveth, Shabtai. *Moshe Dayan.* London: Weidenfeld and Nicholson, 1972.

Tickner, Ann. *Gender in International Relations: Feminist Perspectives on Achieving Global Security.* New York: Columbia Univ. Press, 1992.

Tinh T. Minh-ha. *Woman, Native, Other: Writing Postcoloniality and Feminism.* Bloomington: Indiana Univ. Press, 1989.

Tohidi, Nayereh. "Gender and Islamic Fundamentalism: Feminist Politics in Iran." In *Third World Women and the Politics of Feminism,* ed. Chandra T. Mohanty, Ann Russo, and Lourdes Torres, 51–80. Bloomington: Indiana Univ. Press, 1991.

Toubia, Nahid, ed. *Women of the Arab World: The Coming Challenge*. London: Zed Books, 1988.

Tucker, Judith. *Women in Nineteenth Century Egypt*. New York: Cambridge Univ. Press, 1985.

———. "Ties That Bound: Women and Family in Eighteenth- and Nineteenth-Century Nablus." In *Women in Middle Eastern History*, edited by Nikki R. Keddie and Beth Baron (New Haven: Yale Univ. Press, 1991), 233–253.

Village Voice, 25 Sept. 1990, sec. 1.

Voice of Women, 7 Feb. 1992.

Warnock, Kitty. *Land Before Honour: Palestinian Women in the Occupied Territories*. London: Macmillan, 1990.

Wolfsfeld, Gadi. *The Politics of Provocation: Participation and Protest in Israel*. Albany: State Univ. of New York Press, 1988.

Women's Party Platform, Israel, 1977 (Hebrew).

Woodhull, Winifred, "Unveiling Algeria." *Genders* 10 (Spring 1991): 1–19.

Yediot Achronot, 3 Sept. 1993, 2–3 (Hebrew).

Yediot Achronot, 10 Sept. 1993, 22 (Hebrew).

Yediot Achronot, 24 Sept. 1993. Special Supplement (Hebrew).

Young, Elise. *Keepers of the History: Women and the Israeli-Palestinian Conflict*. New York: Teachers College Press, 1992.

Yuval-Davis, Nira. *Israeli Women and Men: Divisions Behind the Unity*. London: Change Publications, 1982.

———. "The Jewish Collectivity." In *Women in the Middle East*, edited and published by the Khamsin Collective. London: Zed Books, 1987.

Yuval-Davis, Nira and Floya Anthias, eds. *Woman-Nation-State*. London: Macmillan, 1989.

Index

obsession with, 51; militarization
and, 41; as a top priority in Israel,
97, 122–23; peace and, 107;
women's liberation and, 40; Zionist
ideology and, 40
National unity, 33, 96
Negotiations: between Israel and the
PLO, 110, 125
New York Times, 19, 27, 31
Niva, Steve, 167n. 32
Noga, 112
Non-Zionist, 102, 131
Norwegian Institute for Applied Social
Science (FAFO), 19

Oppression: based on gender, race,
class, and national differences, 102;
experiences of, 140–41, 143;
interlocking systems of, 63, 78,
104–5, 108, 118, 122, 129; of
Palestinian women, 78
Organization of Working Mothers, 93
Orientalism, 40, 57
Oslo Accord, 11–12, 19–21. *See also*
Declaration of Principles (DOP);
Gaza and Jericho First plan
Ostrowitz, Rachel, 112, 120, 135,
143–44

Palestine Liberation Organization
(PLO), 5, 21–23, 62, 66–67, 131;
Gulf War and, 81
Palestine National Council (PNC), 62
Palestinian diaspora, 32, 61, 89
Palestinian Federation of Women's
Action Committees (PFWAC), 83
Palestinian leadership, 17, 86
Palestinian self-determination, 32, 86,
104–5
Palestinian state, 32, 87; self-determi-
nation and, 32, 86; territorial

sovereignty and, 32; women and
gender issues and, 78, 80
Palestinian women, 2, 47–55; passive
images of, 38, 57, 91, 135; political
participation of, 70; in relation to
women in other national liberation
movements, 50
Palestinian women prisoners, 38
Palestinian Women's Association
(PWA), 62
Palestinian women's centers, 76–89;
feminist consciousness and, 76
Palestinian women's committees:
during *intifada*, 69–76; prior to
intifada, 65–68
Palestinian women's history, 57
Palestinian women's movement, 7–8,
32; composition of, 69; feminist
consciousness and, 76; national
struggle and, 48
Palestinian Women's Union, 58, 61
Paramilitary organizations, 95
Parents Against Silence, 107–9
Peace (as a women's issue), 104–5
Peace Now, 106–7; Gulf War and, 125;
intifada and, 110, 170–71n. 2
Peace Quilt, 114
Peteet, Julie, 165n. 6
PFLP. *See* Popular Front for the
Liberation of Palestine
PFWAC. *See* Palestinian Federation of
Women's Action Committees
PLO. *See* Palestine Liberation
Organization
PNC. *See* Palestine National Council
Popular committees, 73–75; women's
committees and, 73
Popular Front for the Liberation of
Palestine (PFLP), 67, 131; Oslo
Accord and, 81
Population policies, 34; women's
reproductive roles, 35
PWA. *See* Palestinian Women's
Association

Syracuse Studies on Peace and Conflict Resolution

Harriet Hyman Alonso, Charles Chatfield, and Louis Kriesberg, *Series Editors*

A series devoted to readable books on the history of peace movements, the lives of peace advocates, and the search for ways to mitigate conflict, both domestic and international. At a time when profound and exciting political and social developments are happening around the world, this series seeks to stimulate a wider awareness and appreciation of the search for peaceful resolution to strife in all its forms and to promote linkages among theorists, practitioners, social scientists, and humanists engaged in this work throughout the world.

Other titles in the series include:

An American Ordeal: The Antiwar Movement of the Vietnam Era. Charles DeBenedetti; Charles Chatfield, assisting author
Building a Global Civic Culture: Education for an Interdependent World. Elise Boulding
The Eagle and the Dove: The American Peace Movement and United States Foreign Policy, 1900–1922. John Whiteclay Chambers II
From Warfare to Party Politics: The Critical Transition to Civilian Control. Ralph M. Goldman
The Genoa Conference: European Diplomacy, 1921–1922. Carole Fink
Give Peace a Chance: Exploring the Vietnam Antiwar Movement. Melvin Small and William D. Hoover, eds.
Intractable Conflicts and Their Transformation. Louis Kriesberg, Terrell A. Northrup, and Stuart J. Thorson, eds.
Israeli Pacifist: The Life of Joseph Abileah. Anthony Bing
Mark Twain's Weapons of Satire: Anti-imperialist Writings on the Philippine-American War. Mark Twain; Jim Zwick, ed.
One Woman's Passion for Peace and Freedom: The Life of Mildred Scott Olmsted. Margaret Hope Bacon
Organizing for Peace: Neutrality, the Test Ban, and the Freeze. Robert Kleidman
Peace as a Women's Issue: A History of the U.S. Movement for World Peace and Women's Rights. Harriet Hyman Alonso
Peace/Mir: An Anthology of Historic Alternatives to War. Charles Chatfield and Ruzanna Ilukhina, volume editors
Plowing My Own Furrow. Howard W. Moore
Polite Protesters: The American Peace Movement of the 1980s. John Lofland
The Road to Greenham Common: Feminism and Anti-Militarism in Britain since 1820. Jill Liddington
Timing the De-escalation of International Conflicts. Louis Kriesberg and Stuart Thorson, eds.
Virginia Woolf and War: Fiction, Reality, and Myth. Mark Hussey, ed.
The Women and the Warriors: The United States Section of the Women's International League for Peace and Freedom, 1915–1946. Carrie Foster